THE BEST
AUSTRALIAN
POEMS
2004

THE BEST AUSTRALIAN POEMS 2004

Compiled and Edited by
LES MURRAY

Published by Black Inc.,
an imprint of Schwartz Publishing

Level 5, 289 Flinders Lane
Melbourne Victoria 3000 Australia
email: enquiries@blackincbooks.com
http://www.blackincbooks.com

Introduction and this collection
© Les Murray & Black Inc., 2004.
Individual Poems © retained by the authors.

Every effort has been made to contact the copyright holders
of material in this book. However where an omission has
occurred, the publisher will gladly include acknowledgement
in any future edition.

ALL RIGHTS RESERVED.
No part of this publication may be reproduced, stored in
a retrieval system, or transmitted in any form or by any
means electronic, mechanical, photocopying, recording or
otherwise without the prior consent of the publishers.

ISBN 186 395 2055

Printed in Australia by Griffin Press

Contents

Preface xi

Jordie Albiston	Collectables 1
Lucy Alexander	Trajectories 3
Judith Beveridge	The Dice-Player 5
Tony Birch	At the Creek 7
Elizabeth Blackmore	Dog Bite 9
Mary Bradley	Until Death Do Us Part 10
Kevin Brophy	Life Size 11
Anna Buck	Two Out of Ten 13
Joanne Burns	salt 15
William Carney	Notice 16
Alan Carvosso (Gwen Harwood)	On Wings of Song 18
Gary Catalano	River Song 20
Sherryl Clark	Waitress 22
William C. Clarke	At the Pantheon 23
Hal Colebatch	Red-head with Phosphorus 24
Jennifer Compton	Wave to the Queen 27
Gregory Constantine	The Book 29
Meg Courtney	Sinking Ship 30
Julian Croft	Green Thoughts in a Blue Shade 32

M.T.C. Cronin	The Law of Kindness	34
Luke Davies	Supple	36
Bruce Dawe	Hang in There, Boy	37
Michelle Dicinoski	Lexicon	38
Lucy Dougan	Small Family of Saltimbanques	39
Jane Downing	A True History	40
Tess Driver	Minthe and the Cockroach	42
Stephen Edgar	Entropy Blues	43
Suzanne Edgar	The Loneliness of Salt	45
Russell Erwin	The Cruel Prayer	46
Steve Evans	Left	47
Diane Fahey	Macaws	49
Johanna Featherstone	Tokyo Metro	51
Barbara Fisher	Flight into Egypt	52
Carolyn Fisher	Potato Country	53
William Fleming	Le temps a laissié son manteau	54
John Foulcher	The New Cathedral	55
Lesley Fowler	Reviewing	57
Adrea Fox	Red Felt Hat	58
Jean Frances	Homage to Satie	59
Janine Fraser	Capsicum	60
Katherine Gallagher	At Delphi	61
John Gascoigne	Prodigal	62
Ross Gillett	Taking the Farm Car	64
Peter Goldsworthy	Australia	66

Lisa Gorton	Petrol 67
Alan Gould	The Quick of It 68
Jamie Grant	Emily's Story 70
Robert Gray	Joan Eardley in Catterline 73
Jeff Guess	The Last Anzac 76
Jennifer Harrison	Sideshow History 78
J.S. Harry	Roost 79
Margaret Harvey	Living in M—ls&B—n 81
Graeme Hetherington	Athenian Wolves 83
Matt Hetherington	Triads 84
Barry Hill	A Long Swim 85
Clive James	My Father Before Me 86
John Jenkins	Sydney Road Kebab 88
Kathielyn Job	Bush Versifying 90
Greg Johns	Lachlan Macquarie Inspects Cox's Road 92
Judy Johnson	The Dance 93
Martin R. Johnson	Washing Dishes 95
Paul Kane	Teen Town 96
S.K. Kelen	Hanoi Girls 98
David Kelly	Gang-gangs 101
Joan Kerr	All places are distant from Heaven alike 102
Andy Kissane	Loaves and Days 103
Peter Kocan	Name 105
Mike Ladd	A Vegetative Life 106
Andrew Lansdown	Distress 109

Anthony Lawrence	The Deep Scattering Layer	110
Bronwyn Lea	A Place	112
Cath Lee	The Planets	113
Ray Liversidge	Baudelaire the Bricklayer	114
Kate Llewellyn	The Clairvoyant	116
Miriam W. Lo	Farmgirl Marries	117
Kathryn Lomer	Potato Cutters	119
Yve Louis	Oysters in Gravey	120
Anthony Lynch	Carousel	121
Myron Lysenko	Sex at the Poetry Workshop	122
Ian McBryde	Stalingrad Briefing, 1943	124
Shane McCauley	The Dissolution of a Fox	125
Dennis McDermott	The Up Train	126
Stephen McInerney	At Scots Presbyterian Church, Kiama	127
Graeme Miles	Alternative Daylights	130
Paul Mitchell	Get the Word	132
Rod Moran	My Daughter Reading	134
Ashlley Morgan-Shae	Banana Villanelle	135
Kevin Murray	The Ravenna Job	137
Les Murray	The Cool Green	139
John Augusten Nijjem	Guitar Player. Solea	141
Mark O'Connor	September 11th, 2001	142
Jan Owen	The Hairpin	143
Geoff Page	Algebra	145
Christine Paice	Drama	149

Sheryl Persson	En Espana 150
Dorothy Porter	The Ninth Hour 152
Peter Porter	To Murder Sleep 156
Max Richards	My Wife's Dream 157
David Rowbotham	The Day of Singing Bells 158
Robyn Rowland	This Moon 159
Philip Salom	The Family Fig Trees 161
Andrew Sant	Saxophone in a Pawnbroker's Window 163
Thomas Shapcott	Looking for Ancestors in Limerick 164
Michael Sharkey	Wine 166
Shen	Belief in Ghosts 168
Craig Sherborne	Suburban Confidential 170
Alex Skovron	Dreams of Dead Poets 172
Peter Skrzynecki	The Deep End of the Pond 174
Andrew Slattery	Decision 176
Alan Smith	Kidding Myself in Kuta, Bali: A Pantoum 177
Vivian Smith	Friends and Ancestors 179
Edith Speers	Crow Committee and Raven Review Board 180
Sue Stanford	Rosellas 181
Kathleen Stewart	The Knitting Woman 182
Maurice Strandgard	The King of Prussia Reveals 183
John Tranter	Journey 185

Walter Vivian	A Steam-driven Computer 188
Samuel Wagan Watson	king 190
Chris Wallace-Crabbe	Boleyn, Tourist 191
Meredith Wattison	Mr Waterfeet 192
Alan Wearne	Ballade for Alan Gould 193
Jen Webb	What the Pumpkin Knows 196
John West	Mrs Jackson 197
Petra White	Voyage 198
Lauren Williams	Comic Actor 199
Morgan Yasbincek	Golden Hands 200
Ouyang Yu	Far and Near 201
	Publication Details 203

Preface

Last year's edition of *The Best Australian Poems* presented generous selections of work from a limited number of poets. I have edited anthologies of that kind too, presenting selected Australian poets of earlier times to the British public, but with *The Best Australian Poems 2004* I have chosen to go as wide as possible, limiting each author to a single poem, in order to survey the range and variety of contemporary Australian poetry. Which is a tall order; surveys tell us that over 600,000 Australians, nearly one in thirty of our population, regard creative writing as their main leisure activity. Even moderated by one's experience of intentions versus performance, that probably still means that at least 100,000 people in this country attempt to write poetry in some form. We have no right to assume they are no good at it, either, but few seem to get published, at least on paper. For all I know, vastly more may publish on the internet – I keep right away from that wicked CIA technology. Readings and creative writing classes are certainly outlets for very many. What is striking is that these multitudes buy pitifully few poetry books; you often hear them say, 'Oh I never read other poets: it might affect my own writing.' Magazine editors see the results of this attitude, *en masse* and all the time. My guess is that most of the poets I represent in this book do read other poets, but that's as far as I want to go in risking charges of elitism.

The poems in this book have been selected from work written and/or published over the last year or so up until late August this year. Black Inc., ever generous and obliging, allowed me to survey pretty well all recent individual collections and anthologies – the Water Rat Hotel's *Said the Rat* was a special treasure trove – plus magazines including the marvellous *Blue Dog*. Their office acted as a mail exchange for hundreds of submissions, and they collaborated with me in contacting many Australian poets at home and overseas. Hosts of contributions came to me at home, too, and included some happy accidents, such as the wonderful Bali bombing pantoum of Alan Smith, surely one of Australia's great war poems; he hadn't known the anthology existed and was simply showing his poem to me. Because people had usually pre-selected their offerings, I was able to say a lot more Yes than one gets to say in ordinary magazine editing, and where I had to turn work down, I hope I always remembered to wish the author better luck with next year's editor. Older-style academic magazines were hard to locate, even in university libraries; I kept hearing It's at the binders, or It's out on loan, or We don't get that one. Suburban Willoughby Library in Sydney outdid them all. I also found comparatively little poetry in the critical journals, hardly more than in the newspapers, from which I clipped some late poems up till the end of August, as the last contributions also landed in our roadside mailbox.

There are poets I have missed, and I am sorry. I know perhaps half of the poets represented, but often only by name. So far as I know, the youngest contributor to get in is Gregory Constantine, a schoolboy now seventeen years old. I have no idea who is the oldest, but two at least have gone beyond age: Gary Catalano and Gwen Harwood, recently deceased, are represented by poems of theirs published within the time-limits of the book. I have not included any biographical or (God spare us!) auto-critical notes; hardly any of the contributors offered any. If a writer has any saving modesty, such pars can be a misery to compose; if they are immodest, the results are mostly embarrassing. And most readers probably ignore them. If they want real information about an author whose work has interested them, many have websites on the net, or can be approached personally. These days, when I am asked that intrusive old question about my Influences, I reply truthfully that I learned by far the most from

Anthologus, presenter of good poems by many hands; he has a reprobate indifference to careers. All the poems in this book have given me pleasure. My hope is that they will all please the common reader, that ideal civilian who luckily resides outside poetry circles and isn't beholden to us or set to police us. If we can't delight that reader, we are trapped inside a loop with our hundred thousand fellow dreamers and their apparent reading habits.

Les Murray
Bunyah, NSW

Collectables

... can never be catalogued or appraised ...
—Orson Welles

I collect mistakes and faulty prime numbers she says about herself. I collect quotes and jokes and dreams like Freud himself he says. I used to collect foreign stamps till I gave them all to the damp Italian girl nobody spoke to she says. A prime philatelic mistake he says. My collection of coins echoes each continent

as well as the nether countries she says. My matchbox covers are close to complete he says. I tried to collect cigarette packs but prevention prevailed in the end she says. He says you can always take it up again. My snowdomes serve as my homes-away-from-home she says. That's how I view my Disneyana he says.

I have a collection of personality defects dating back to Christ she says. Well my ten mint commandments are carved out of bakelite made by the Romans he says. She says I possess enough swizzle-sticks to fill your Studebakers. I'll pull them out with tin Civil War men he says. Will you trade your range of Lionel trains

for my wind-up carousel causes she says. Plus your display of Victorian hysteria he says. I could let that go if you throw in your horde of Victrolas and vintage hymns she says. Then hand over all your ornamental issues he says. She says if and when you give up your entire vocabulary of isms. In your dreams of Xanadu

he says. She says your heart. And everything therein.
(It is said that Citizen Kane was possibly a woman.)

Jordie Albiston

Trajectories

To cross the rope's umbilical line
the acrobat's feet must go two by two
ahead of him without his excitable
tightrope heart hopping against his sternum,
practising with oversized wings.

Did Icarus question his father
about those wings, as they stole
wax from the workshop?
Quietening the birds with enormous flight,
Crete a tear in the sea's glow below him;
above him, the sky's yawning dare to his youth
calling him closer and then closer
to that eye of heat.

It was long before the moment wax
gave in to flame, that his fall began.

The acrobat feels his foot miss
a wingbeat. Sweat starts out
of his forehead, candle-drops,
a plume. Below him, his sea,
his audience's eyes, points of light, shifting.
He has no choice but
to give gravity his resistance,
the wings of fear flex again
in his throat, though now
the heat is all his own.

Where does the legend end?
The lion, Daedalus,
mane spread out like fire,
scans the horizon's line for
the relics of the fallen.

As if he can see some soft arc
in the myth, like an arrow in
the air's invisibility.
A trajectory, like an anchor's rope,
tracing the fallen to their landing places.
The only route, gravity's choice
for the body; a spring of safety net,
twang of spine.

Lucy Alexander

The Dice-Player

I've had my nose in the ring since I was nine.
I learned those cubes fast: how to play a blind
bargain; how to empty a die from my palm
and beguile by turns loaded with prayers —
then sleight of hand. Ten or fifteen years
and you get wrists like a tabla-player's, jaws

cut and edged by the knuckles and customs
of luck and deception. The fun's in sham,
in subterfuge, in the eyes smoking out
an opponent's call. I let my thumb stalk
each die, get to know which edge might
damage probability's well-worn curves.

See, all dice are cut on the teeth of thugs,
liars and raconteurs. I've concocted calls
those dealing in risk and perfidy, bluff or
perjury, would envy. But I've never stolen
or coveted dice fashioned from agate
or amber, slate or jasper, or from

the perfumed peach stones of distant shores.
Some think fortunes will be won with dice
made from the regurgitated pellets of owls;
or from the guano of seabirds that ride only
the loftiest thermals. I've always had faith
in the anklebones of goats, in the luxated

kneecaps of mountain-loving pugs. Look,
I've wagered all my life on the belief that
I can dupe the stars, subtend the arcs, turn
out *scrolls, louvers, pups, knacks, double
demons* — well, at least give a game rhythm.
I know there'll always be an affliction

of black spots before my eyes, that my face
has its smile stacked slightly higher on
the one side, that the odds I'm not a swindler
are never square. But, Sir, when some rough
justice gets me back again to the floor,
then watch me throw fate a weighted side.

Judith Beveridge

At the Creek

for Simon Ortiz

I.
my brother warms his skin
on the worn slabs of stone
as we rest with our bodies
and wait for the painted fish
to swim upstream to us

he tells me I must be gone
before the strangers come for us
with crosses and beads
turning our souls to prayer

he tells me I must become
down feathered and winged
the bird of all journeys
with an eye for night

it is time to fly
and I must go, he tells me
before they come for me
with lead and chains

II.
at the creek the lost boys
are chromed and roaming
wearing tin-men faces
and saddened shadows hidden
beneath the body of the boy-angel

bloated and beaten
in blood and water

I call across the bruised sky
to my brother's heart
he does not know me
with his beauty in hiding
he forgets himself
and turns away from me

at the water's edge I wait
with Simon by my side
he asks me without words –
'when they tell you that
your brother does not exist
how do you feel?'

Tony Birch

Dog Bite

my dog did this I grab my arm to keep it shut no blood
but from the holes ooze yellow worms of fat you got rid
of the dog of course a question from the stern intern as he
patches and sews the greyness of shock spares me from
   answering

After the stitching my arm sprouted black whiskers.

Elizabeth Blackmore

Until Death Do Us Part

His first punch
took her by surprise.
The second was deflected
by her gold wedding ring
the force of the blow
distorting the circle –
'until death do us part'.

The first punch
blackened her eye
the second ended their marriage
bruised flesh was the notification
case adjourned
for a long twenty years.

She shied away from surprises
gave her love to the kids.
He grew old with his anger
balled tight like a fist in his pocket.

Mary Bradley

Life Size

*on passing a statue of Father Brosnan outside the
Brosnan Centre in Brunswick*

Outside the welfare centre
a bronze priest stands on the street,
one cold hand shaking
hands with the air
or with an apparition invisible to me.

He is a man without art
a true saint wrinkled to a realism
his God must envy.
He is blank inside of course
despite the over-friendly smile
and open palm of greeting.

Barely five foot six or seven;
paunch, jowls; neck jammed into holy collar
and a black shirt skew-whiff
untouched by mirror or woman,
he grins at a square inch of air
and his hand startles me each time I pass

on my way to the pool next door,
my mind on undressing
and dipping my body in the rectangular
font of water blue as paint and cold as metal
as real as my hand but still
a sign of something else.

I want to believe the bronze priest
goes inside at night
as tired as the street's cockroaches and mice
but still grinning because that is his last miracle,
most famous mood
all the way down to the hand formed to grip mine.

But in truth he is bolted to the asphalt,
his feet in a surprising pair of moccasins,
knees and cheeks burning gold
like his luminous hand
stuck out as if to bluff Saint Peter at the Gate,
grin showing teeth too much like dentures,
eyes locked on nothing forever.

No ideals here, nothing but the thing
that insists on being.
The bronze priest counts the dust
particles in the air of Brunswick
for me and you
as he waits the infinite wait of the good at heart.

Kevin Brophy

Two Out of Ten

When they took away the schoolhouse
wisteria straddling the verandah
fell, its back broken
showering blue petals and bees
into hydrangeas acidic with tea leaves
teachers' wives had thrown there
since 1851.

It took a front-end loader,
two trucks, a day
and four smokoes
to break the house in three
and haul bloodwood slabs
and corrugated iron away.

When the cortege passed
rooms where children had lain
(scraped knees or headache eased
by aspirin and blowfly hum;
clean knickers handed out,
hollow teeth painted with clove oil)
were exposed; shadowy
corners sliced as if by the Blitz.

French doors flapped.
The chalk dust ghost
realising dispossession
sought to haunt
stone steps leading up
to nothing.

The whiskered lemon tree
with nowhere to hide
wept little green fruit
bitterly, took a
detention, forgot its lunch
stood outside
for the rest of the century.

Anna Buck

salt

all day the life
continued to climb
out of you shakily
and mumbling as if the ladder
was too rickety, old, as if it
might collapse at any second;
but as usually happens in these
situations it reached the top when we
least expected and suddenly it was
gone, your body didn't crumple with
its departure but simply lay there, neat
and succinct in its new pyjamas indicating
a 'fait accompli'; i could feel the warm
breeze of you across the ceiling and then
on the small balcony you lingered a moment
as we sipped fresh hot tea which i still haven't
finished and i lit a cigarette, o its tip's red
spark; then you took off like the arc of a golf
ball on the links just over the road through
the deep green hedge with its arcane verses, and
you hitched your new future to the whoosh
of a big salty wave across bondi's rooftops; when i
cleared the cold drawers to pack all your clothes
up, and i unplugged your phone i inhaled
your voice

Joanne Burns

Notice

Ronni dies on Bondi beach.
He dies because he's out of reach.
Four lawmen found his craze too much
their pistols kept them out of touch.

A bloke thrown off a train in Brissie
lost the plot, he's not us is he!
In riot gear, the Force, it comes
dispels our pain, with capsicum.

The local youth gangs run the Mall
the papers tell us, after all.
'What's needed is a firmer hand'
(more of the same, you understand).

Eleven million bucks, today
go out to help the Coppers play
to win. No questions, though we squeal
they'll shoot us down with *Glock* and schpiel.

The Premiers turn their backs on John
'But, what of guns? …' he cries, '… Come on!'
The shooters rifle the Accord
and mock the massacre, dear Lord …

And towns divide on Rich and Poor
the 'have nots' and their 'haves-in-law'.
No bridge connects their common ties
which 'neath the glossy surface lies

You drive a city four-wheel-drive.
You live, while others can't survive
Protected in your cage of steel
So safe, but is your safety real?

We build our walls of wealth and brick –
effective, cost-efficient, slick –
to keep the other half at bay
from what we've earned; that's what we say

But streets of walls and iron curtain
rise and fall, that's ever certain.
Construct your fences, watch and frown
– they're words, and words can tear them down.

William Carney

On Wings of Song

Earth unlocks wings, flowers, leaves, old jewels of sunlight.
In murmuring crowds the Sunday pilgrims throng
to a summer concert in the public gardens.
Blue air walks between lime and elder, singing,
as the band begins to play 'On Wings of Song'.

Under the English trees still thick with summer
two lovers walk; no longer young, they see
yellow invade the pure, harsh green of lime trees,
and breathe as with a single inspiration
the riches of late flowers. Light's clarity

can spare them nothing. Faces are more abstract,
flesh wears the gravity that pulls it down.
Each sees a flawless other still, erasing
years, years, when absence simplified to anguish
kept them awkward and truthful, in their own

prisons of memory drinking the sublime
love-fire of *this must be*. At last, though late,
they stroll upon green-mantled graves, abandoning
as it were leaf by leaf their lofty anguish,
content to pass unnoticed here, to wait

and learn what time will tell. Uprooted headstones
lean upon flowering vines. The lovers read
what time has told, flaking memorials:
The First White Child sleeps in its charnel cradle,
many lovers are dead, and dead indeed.

Round them, enmeshed in change, a city alters.
New buildings fit in holes ripped overhead
by steel and glass, but here the lovers, carried
on wings of song, rest in a blossoming garden
at peace, one evening closer to the end.

Alan Carvosso (Gwen Harwood, 1920–1995)

River Song

When the sky's all grey
and the water's brown
I spend every day
on the Pont Marie
and dream that I live
on a flat-topped barge.

River run clear,
river run slow;
take me downstream
to the Pont Mirabeau.

When the water looks
like *café au lait*
and the rain comes down
both night and day
I wish that I lived
on a flat-topped barge.

River run clear,
river run slow;
take me downstream
where all lovers go.

With my cat on one knee
and my bird on the other
I'll drift downstream
and pretend it's summer
and live forever
on a flat-topped barge.

River run clear,
river run slow;
take me downstream
to the Pont Mirabeau.

Gary Catalano (1947–2002)

Waitress

you grow monstrous feet
red and swollen, soles on fire
toes gasping for air

eight hours of balancing
four plates of 'special of the day'
up your arm

bending over the gluttons
at Table 4 who demand
extra rolls 3 times

crockery speeds around the room
sometimes as much food goes back
as comes out

Table 8 order more wine
which they won't drink but the staff
will after work

when it's busy time races by
and you don't get stuck with
polishing silver

Table 9 leave their coffee with cigarette
butts floating like charred turds
and you're no longer hungry

Sherryl Clark

At the Pantheon

a postcard from Rome

What spiritual catch can be exacted
from a visit to the ancient city
where devotion's currency
weakens against time's desertion,
shuffles in halting caterpillar queues,
buffeting crowds in contrary flow
and it's all thumbs through guidebook pages,
minuscule designations on map mazes,
falling lost in bent and sultry streets
which change their names along their lenient ways?

Until I found that place
where light led my gaze aloft
to a fontanelle of stone
open always to admit
sky and rain and sun and snow
falling softly, softly falling,
equipping me to hook shy morsels
swimming there
holy in that apprehended air.

William C. Clarke

Red-head with Phosphorus

Red-haired girl in a white bikini
who he saw for the first time aglow
on a launch moored in a Rottnest bay
twenty-five years ago,

inviting them up from their sailing dinghy
to share the owner's champagne:
as the green water lapped in the sunlight,
as they bobbed on the mooring chain.

He was, he recalls, a painful mess
and she was sweet and kind,
both certainly more than he deserved,
and more than he'd looked to find.

Quaffing champagne in the cockpit,
and diving off the bow.
It would be perfect, the owner remarked
if they could stop time now.

And she, and his friend, and the owner
laughed together in the sun.
He was the moody, silent dork,
just trying to offend no one.

Later they took the dinghy
and they sailed in the moonlit bay,
He remembers that phosphorescent time
as if it were yesterday,

or yesternight, to be precise
as they sailed through the easterly blow
with the launches and yachts at their anchors,
and the phosphorus aglow,

with the dinghy's bows splitting the dark,
and the easterly blowing warm,
his friend lying drunk on the bottom-boards,
and she snuggled under his arm.

And lights on the island and anchored boats
dwindled and left them the stars.
The waves rushed in cool green fire
and the sheets were taut as bars.

A wonderful night, he thought as they sailed
(I said more than he'd looked to find).
He'd never forget it, he thought, and he had
no more than that in his mind.

The moon slid down and he sadly turned,
headed back and the rocks slid past.
They came ashore by the army base
and he thought it was over at last.

They waded ashore through that green fire
when the night was otherwise black.
When he daringly turned and kissed her
she, amazingly, kissed him back.

When they'd dug the anchor into the sand
and pulled the boat up the shore,
He found to his astonishment
that that night held a good deal more.

That was a night, whatever's come since,
(people and pleasure and pain)!
Oh! Pocket-sized red-headed Venus,
who put him together again!

Hal Colebatch

Wave to the Queen

The last woman in the world to ride side-saddle
smiled at me from the screen
at the Kinema in Kilbirnie.
I stood
for the neat brown gelding and the woman in the red coat and
    divided skirt.
It's what we did.

Lofty mothers in frocks and hats and gloves, lippy and powder,
    a dab of Coty,
had stopped in the street to put their heads together –
    Coronation! Queen!
Golden coach! White horses! White maidens with white
    flowers in their hair!
A girl with a velvet and ermine train turning into something
    rare.

The whole world as we knew it was watching her, but now I
    know
she had a moment of solitude as she became the thing she had
    to be
the camera didn't look, there was a break in transmission,
    verboten.

The old man in the gold frock bowed and stepped backwards.
He had touched her with the oil and her task had entered her.

The organ thundered all stops out and boys, like my brother,
sang like angels with frills around their necks.
They gave her heavy things with heavy names,
the orb, the mace, the crown.

A nutter with a starting pistol
firing on the streets of London
startled your neat brown gelding
retired at twenty, called Burmese.
You kept your seat side-saddle
as he shied you bent to speak to him
patted him on the neck to settle him
looked up and saw, as he made a canter step,
the – *is this it?* – the – *this is it!* – and then
– *this isn't it!* – Rode on with your entourage.

Jennifer Compton

The Book

The big book is like a piece of old rugged wood,
For it shaves away to reveal its beautiful story.

Gregory Constantine

Sinking Ship

She could still see the blood
soaking through the thick fabric
The red coat like camouflage
though the blood's hue was redder.

As she sat on the cold hard seat,
she could feel the warm
spread in her thighs.
And when she feared
it might drip
from the back of her chair,
she'd raised her hand,
stood up and ran out.

At home she's on a couch
that's lined with garbage bags.
The blood rising up around her
like some kind of sinking ship,
watching it make its way
up to her elbows,
the pool quite deep
where the weight of her
body sits.

Her husband paces
and clears his throat
as their doctor stands in the kitchen
tapping a staccato toe.

A stony silence
when their twelve-year-old daughter
comes home from school
and gleans her mother
now a strange shade of white,
who lacks the strength to round the
corners of her mouth.

A sight so shocking that it causes
the child to prattle about hockey
and how muddy she is.

The child is glued to the carpet
when her mother asks for a kiss hello.

And suddenly sirens in the sickly quiet house.

And as the woman is helped to her feet,
a magenta swell crashes
over the edges of the couch,
splashing behind her as she's ushered away.

'We'll be back soon,' she says
extending a shaky paw to the child's cheek,
the seas rising as water pours
down her pallid face.

'Mum ...' moans the tear-damp daughter
shipwrecked at the end of her bed,
fear whistling in her ears as she waits
for the click of the front door.

Meg Courtney

Green Thoughts in a Blue Shade

Beach Hotel, 4 p.m., 10 August 2001

No more work
but still things to do:
I almost wrote
'you sit in a bar'
when I realised
I was no longer second person,
I now own myself:
'I' at the centre of things
unpaid and unemployed at last
the world in pawn each day
as I redeem all those lost hours
and watch that other time outside
9 2 5.
The quiet streets where a bomb
has dropped at 10 a.m.
and wiped out all the young and fit
with the botulism of work
when you, that is, I
can hear the birds because the rush-hour
traffic has passed:
where the clouds seem suddenly closer
and the sea a more brilliant blue
as I sit at the bar and watch the surf
tireless worker on the beach,
and wonder how those waves of energy
propagate across the globe
and end here dissipated in work.

But 'work' has purpose hasn't it?
And if it has, isn't it
the heat death of the universe,
agent of undoing?
Even now with the first signs of Spring on the terrazzo
where the couples sink Friday afternoon's first white wine
and celebrate rest and release,
as they flirt and look into each other,
the busy swell erodes our lives as we make others
who one day will sit in idleness and think
against the stream of things,
or squeeze their eyes to see
to the other side where energy
sits still as a ship on the horizon
so far from consciousness it doesn't move.
Yet there are still things to do
before utter silence freezes the frame,
something that 'I' would do
and 'you' would never dare,
like write this poem
incomplete and unfocused as the world
in which energy surges through words
and lines of waves build up
and smash in pleasure at their ruin.

Julian Croft

The Law of Kindness

To produce nothing
But yourself
Is the kindest action
For the universe

When pushed
To swing like a little door
That others
May pass through

To be an accident
Of the world
So that even your name
Loses its grip

Like a sleeping cat
In the flowers
You can ignore
The lizard and the bird

How kind is the sun
To those
With enough to do
Just sitting around

How kind
The happiness of cucumbers
And the nest full
With spotty eggs

And as if no more
Than the residue
Of a dream
You might murmur

To produce nothing
But myself
Is all the universe
Expects today

M.T.C. Cronin

Supple

And the sun is everywhere
And the air is filled with pollen
And all the bees weighed down with light
Are golden where the leaves have fallen.

The sidewalk soft with petals.
The air is wet with blossom;
It was frankly hard to comprehend
How all your youth and grace, so lissome,

So supple, could gather in the one body.
The light comes through your hair
As if your hair were light and nothing but:
You shake it out, set fire to the air.

Luke Davies

Hang in There, Boy

O you America, with your wise-cracks, canned applause,
what did we ever do
to deserve you?
                  You,
with your rich clientele,
creator and demolisher of demons, semi-professional
exorcisor, whose all-too-folksy glib
ambassadors so rarely speak the tongues
of countries where the refugee camps
are pitched on dusty misery.
                          O you America,
to whom can we look but you
– voted year after year the World's
Most Popular Enemy, brave in the field, pusillanimous often
in foreign policy, too big by far
to always get it right, although invariably sure
this time you'll thread your bullish way
through the china-shop without the smashed porcelain?

O you America, whom we hate to love, singer
of beautiful songs, peace-dreaming child
of Salem and Sodom, would-be flexi-time world-saviour,
   twirling still,
like a majorette's baton your trusty hi-tech Sam Colts
in God knows what back-alleys (as though we had not long
   since run
quite out of West in this confused confusing
global Jerusalem ...).
                  O you America.

Bruce Dawe

Lexicon

I don't love you
for your beauty
alone,
but also for your large
vocabulary.

When you say
emporium and
brouhaha instead of
shops and a
fistfight it
really turns me on.

Tell me all the synonyms
for smitten
and I'll tell you what I am.

Michelle Dicinoski

Small Family of Saltimbanques

The small family of saltimbanques
occupies one corner of the dance hall every Saturday.
The oldest girl moves with the same self-sufficiency
that all her family possesses. She walks an edge
of holding something back and then giving it fully.
The younger ones sit in a circle with their mother.
Her body made each one no more or less beautiful than the
    next,
as if she had chided patiently before their births:
now do not outshine the one before you.
It could be a family credo, this democracy of looks.
In their little circle they eat and play, practising a patience
that certain beggars own. Nothing is too showy, everything
    eked out.
Their mother watches them with a poised neutrality.
She is with them the same way her oldest child dances.
At any moment she is tuned to another order, to almost
imperceptible openings. The colour of skin
beneath her eyes, a feather-blue in forest light.

Lucy Dougan

A True History

You know the troopers were sent to catch him
that Ned shot them, one Kennedy unarmed and in surrender
Know when his gasping breath pained their sensibilities too far,
Kelly shot him again as you would a fallen horse –
a dumb sick animal, not the husband of a wife
Under the eye of the laughing jackass Sergeant Kennedy died
and the bullet ricochets still through my breast
           ripping out my heart to bleed

But, no, I must and have put out my anger
For it had crowded my heart as tight as a coffin
pushing the love I'd known beyond the border of memory
To love my Kennedy again,
I have had to find a way to forgive his killer
a man who had wrong done to him some say
a man who did great wrong
           But just a man

The judge said he apportioned a just punishment
still I understood the weight of the heartache
for those left behind by the hangman's noose.
And yet, my own heart is not so big to understand all from
    that day:
why I have had to watch as you make him your Hero
The bluff beard, sharp eyes, outlandish armour
were your thousand words to make a star for your legend
               while the victims are mute beneath the sod

While I, Bridget Tobin that was
Bridget Kennedy but briefly married
must keen in the small corners you'll allow
        Such is the life he left me

                    Jane Downing

Minthe and the Cockroach

Minthe travelled, like the cockroach,
from Asia to Egypt, cleansing
stinking breath arising from
the corruption of the mouth.
Jealous Persephone turned her
to a crawling plant. Pluto
softened the spell, giving Minthe
the sweetest smell when crushed.

And so it came to pass that Ancients
fried the cockroach in oil and garlic
to cure their indigestion, dried and
powdered it, made it into tea, while
it multiplied, scrabbling, emigrating,
six hairy legs on each and eighteen knees.
The creature lives without its head
but cannot live with mint.

Mint, the aphrodisiac of Arabs,
stirs bodily lust; deters fleas.
Mint helps women with swollen,
sagging breasts; mint and salt help
those bitten by mad dogs;
but best of all, this herb of hospitality
when strewn in rodent-ridden places
keeps cockroaches away.

Tess Driver

Entropy Blues

Tic in my jaw has slackened.
I'm high on feverfew.
I'd sleep, but in my dreams I'm black and blue.

I put a detective on you
To find out where you went.
Said he found your bus ticket by the monument.

'I got it here in my satchel.
Then I traced her to the door
She entered with an eligible bachelor.

Had to peek in through the transom
Just to make sure it was her.'
And him? 'You're handsome. He was handsomer.'

Well, you used to live in Sweden.
You can play bridge and whist.
I might have known you would prove a hedonist.

Me, I'm out of date as Pliny
Or a two-string guitar.
The world's postmodern and nonlinear.

I read of the strange attractor,
Wondered who that might be,
Thinking of you all day at the factory.

Oh, I'm desperate and I'm livid,
I need something to spend.
The boss's already blown my dividend.

I asked the bishop one day
If you'd broken the golden rule.
He said, 'I don't know *you* from Sunday school.'

Saw my lawyer for a second
Opinion. He says I'm right –
I think; his talk can be so recondite.

I feel so drained and puny,
Should book myself a hearse.
You couldn't look better if you were Miss Universe.

Now the ship's pulling up its anchor
And the dockside's full of grief.
Had to give away my second-best handkerchief.

The air is supersonic.
My head is slow as wool.
I seem to be someone else in the chronicle.

Sun reignites in the water
Flames the firemen douse.
The sky is redder than a slaughterhouse.

Now that's got to mean disaster.
Let me quote the chief of police:
'Confusion now hath made his masterpiece.'

Stephen Edgar

The Loneliness of Salt

Wanting the comfort of waves,
my aunt looks out to sea.
From inside the cocoon car
she stares and stares,
waiting for salt solace.

She has left her cold house,
her days of filing the office,
nights with just the wireless;
no more Father, not even Mother.
Home, unfit for human consumption,
is dry as old bread in her mouth.

I could say she's a bone-thin beast
dragging slow feet to the salt-lick,
back leg lame;
no brisk wife to grab a pinch of salt
or brush away specks.
If she ever threw salt over her left shoulder
it has not kept away bad luck.

This woman, my never asked-for aunt,
has driven through Sunday
to sit, very still, on The Front
and stare at salt-spray sea
till the soothe of it enters into her.

Suzanne Edgar

The Cruel Prayer

'What's that dear? Can't hear you.
Get me my coat. No. I'm going out.
Yes. That's right. That's right. Yes.
No. I'm going out today. Going out.
What's that dear? Can't hear you.
No, he hasn't come today.
My hat. Get me my hat. What's that?
Can't hear you dear. I'm cold.
Get me my hat dear. I'm so cold.'
As she lies bared on a bed,
Talking to her daughter,
Talking to the ceiling.

Or chants 'Our Father / which art / in Heaven'
Over and over. Over and over.
Over and over.
                    Is this prayer?
Or sound roped by rhythm,
Each syllable as desperate as hand-over-hand
Defence against a flood?

Then is silent.
Bewilderment too is beyond her
As she's hoisted in a sling
And wheeled along a corridor,
Just as they do a drip-stand.
Her nightgown caught above her waist,
The strap creased up into her crotch
Like a g-string.

Russell Erwin

Left

one morning the body chooses
a different outfit
leaves the suit on the hanger
leaves the front door open
turns left rather than right
at the usual corner
and never returns to the old job
old house old family
who told it to do this?
what words were used?
what spell?

there it goes
into the next suburb
by nightfall it will be
almost beyond the city
as if blind to all previous logic
or finally seeing through it
who's responsible?
not me says the mind
I'm just along for the ride
any steps past this one
haven't been invented yet
the body makes it up
as it goes along
it can happen to anyone

it is 1965
my father steps out
into a sunny August morning
his body hasn't told him yet
that today is a left turn day
that we'll never see him again
his suit already dead in the wardrobe
his kids still asleep
his wife in the shower
and everything behind him
as he approaches the corner

Steve Evans

Macaws

So this is what parrots become
when they let themselves go,
allow excess to roost in their souls –

breasts in sunglasses-strength saffron;
blue wings an untidy archive of
noon to first star; old-jewellery-box

tarnish on ragged wedding train …
Huddled in nit-picking love
they touch beak-coloured tongues;

drape swathes of plumage against
each other; in amplified propinquity,
air pinions touchy as radar.

Jesters more than saints, yet
at times a piercing probity,
the hint of immutable intentions

as heartbeats rock long-dead branches.
Near dusk, a royal progress from perch
to sequestered cage – mobile bric-a-brac

colonising a Victorian parlour
with shrieks that could wake the dead,
or scold them back to sleep:

this gorgeous waddling into the dark,
the light on their feathers undressed by it,
zebra-lidded eyes noting you,

the exotic, without condescension;
wisely adapted, fantastically sane,
lacking only a rainforest.

Diane Fahey

Tokyo Metro

Thigh high in uniforms,
a posse of pigeon-toed
girls flirt through text
messages & languid blinks.
Palm-sized grannies fold
into bows & nap alongside
loyal businessmen who store
years of sleep in bags
beneath their eyes.

Everyone dreams between
stops on these overpopulated
trains – silent as
chopsticks on rice.

Johanna Featherstone

Flight into Egypt

The family is resting in the shade
of an unconvincing tree,
the radiant child on his mother's lap,
the paniered donkey grazing.
And what is Joseph doing?
He reclines upon the ground,
chin propped on easeful elbow.
He is reading.

We are used to Mary's book,
her study interrupted
by an angel with a lily
and a message,
but Joseph's whole demeanour
suggests that he is reading
for pleasure.

What made the painter veer
so far from the expected?
Questioned, I suppose
he said, of course,
the saint is deep
in holy scripture.

But that pose?
The disarming sense
that he is unaware
of great events unfolding,
so lost is he in story.

Barbara Fisher

Potato Country

Spring rain left dams full as bellies after chips for tea;
summer pumps a fun-fair of fire-hose pressure over paddocks,
the whirligigs arc high, hit sky and soak a green crowd.
Fields are fanned cooler than degrees which crack ground
oven-ready for potato moths, the six-hourly switch
of tractors and pipes relentless as class-sorting at the factory.

Round here on hot days cattle wilt near fence lines for drizzle
to drift their way, farm dogs lap full ditches and high winds
   peel spindrift
off curved-curtain rails of water like shifts of skin. Everyone
   knows
everyone, the taste of a raw rural economy and, never mash
   a Pink-eye,
keep Kennebecs for roasting and Dutch Creams for family
   dinners
where talk revolves around fixed prices or the need to diversify.

Butter-fingered harvesters whine 'wide-loads' up country roads
to chew through acres, spitting spuds into cock-eyed trucks
that slant down. Drivers in battered hats tip the same finger to
   neighbours
or strangers and at every dip or turn you'll see generations
of potato growers in revolutions of the irrigator's spray, plumes
that hang around for seconds before the spectres walk away.

Carolyn Fisher

Le temps a laissié son manteau

translated from the French of Charles d'Orléans

The season's laid aside his shroud
Of ice and sleet all shivery,
And's now decked out in finery
Of sunny skies without a cloud.

All beasts and birds, as they're endowed,
Hoot, chirp, or bray out – variously –
The season's laid aside his shroud!

See too the rivers done right proud
In the crinkliest of livery –
All repoussé and filigree.
The whole world has been freshly scoured!
The season's laid aside his shroud.

William Fleming

The New Cathedral

The new cathedral
is a corridor
and a thousand tiny rooms.

Nothing is fixed
in the new cathedral,
the rooms shift and are scattered
as if the saints were shuffling cards.

The angels in cages
of lead-lined glass
are flapping about.

Icons are everywhere:
the ecstasy of weddings, the heavenly families.

In the new cathedral
to receive the host
is to open one's lips
on the most luscious kiss.

The priests
of the new cathedral
are weeping in the confessional.
Their whispered sins
have become our breath.

There is a gift shop
at the heart of the new cathedral
but no change is given.
Everything is cheaper by the dozen.

We buy our lives
and swap them.
We tell each other stories of salvation.

There is dust
in the pulpit,
dust on the lectern.

There are no funerals in the new cathedral.
The dead are otherwise.

A hymn is shuffling
in the shadows
of the new cathedral.
It is quietly singing to itself.

Prayers gather in the rafters
like swallows preening.

No services are held
in the new cathedral
for the priests cannot be distracted,
they are crafting their liturgies of elegance and splendour.

In the new cathedral
nothing happens,
we wait on the mercy of God.

John Foulcher

Reviewing

When I start to read he's sitting
where he always sits,
at the head of the table, and I'm at the side
in my dead mother's place.
He's asked me to read a review
out loud, his eyes are failing.
In the review I talk about language
and how saying 'she'
not 'he', has changed my world.
Although I'm speaking clearly, he gets up
and moves to my side
of the table, quietly, and leans on it
with both hands,
balancing.
I glance up. He's very still, and staring
at the blank wall
to hear my words. (Doesn't he know why I write
like this? Doesn't he see that this
is about him? His years of yelling
and hitting the table. The way things jumped.)
He moves closer,
one hand still on the table, the other
on the back of my chair.
I read on, trying to keep one eye
on him, and then
he pats my hair
'Good,' he says. 'Stop now.'

Lesley Fowler

Red Felt Hat

She sits crowned by the weight
of eighty-two years
a red felt hat
the Carlton restaurant moves quietly
between academia and motherhood
she identifies with a baby in the corner
she waves to attract a mind on the way in
while hers wanders between World War II
and the broken fingernail on her left hand
I cut the crusts off her bread
with the same precision as the mother
at the table next to me
we look and smile
at the inversion of roles
how time has twisted us around
until I am not her daughter and she is not my mother
conversation is aimless
until the knife drops from the table
cutting through the labyrinth of her thoughts
her hand touches mine
our eyes meet
she asks 'Are you happy?'

Adrea Fox

Homage to Satie

(1886–1925)

Lone wolf   An eccentric
The recluse who never allowed
another in his dwelling

After his death it was reported
he collected umbrellas   dozens
were found in his Parisian apartment
piled in capacious wardrobes
mildew-embroidered between the folds
Readers smiled as the story went on
to mention hoards of matchboxes
in which he'd stored scraps of paper
whimsical ideas perhaps
for his singular compositions
with a blissful disregard for bar lines

But I listen now   transfixed
by his heartrending piano music
and see clearly the slant
of winter sunlight on yellowed keys
and his fingers forming precisely
the third Piece in the Shape of a Pear

Jean Frances

Capsicum

square jawed tending to jowl
flushed ruddy skin looping under
the chin the set of her

there is no denying her this
she is cook here in our kitchen
she has brought capsicum

and no complain you will
eat and you will like this is proper
cooking this is our traditional

fruit of her labour this is her
pride her joy lopping the tops off
caps those jaunty green

gnome peaks doffed
while she does her stuff the red cheeks
fat with herbs with spiced rice

you will never taste anything
like it never anywhere else only here
in our kitchen she cook

for us her tomato sauce
her jaw square as capsicum and
you will like it or else

Janine Fraser

At Delphi

Clouded Yellows, Red Admirals, others I cannot name
weaving in and out of bindweed, daisies, buttercups.
They've flown over wide sea-stretches
to reach these wild grasses, tombs and ruins.

I breathe the scented air, feel the sky's silk,
there for the taking. I can almost unknot
my unhappiness, see how its underside
is the impossible love
I've carried all this way
like spare, necessary baggage.

Can I ungrip it, leave it here
for random gods to give one last blessing?
I hear your voice urging me on
to walk through this
steady fire of butterflies.

Katherine Gallagher

Prodigal

Do not raise a fattened calf
or slaughter anything on my behalf:
I will not come back, a penitent.

Indulged so long in swill
that you thought I had surrendered my will:
my belly filled, a familiar bulge.

I walk out on the web of prospects
withheld as threat.
You wave them grimly about,
an attempt at traction in the absence of love.
My brother holds on to his investment.

I rehearsed the magic words
that would sever us:
twin black hearses, borne in different directions.
I get out of my coffin.

Of course there is more rejoicing
over the returned prodigal:
there is nowhere left to go,
from now on he will toe the line.

I will not give you that satisfaction.

Now I am a loose man, trading on my beauty.
Your genetics have a use.
Nothing is beneath me
as long as I am not under you.

The fat anaconda nestled at your bosom
wakes from its agony of digestion
and bellies away from
the one woman it will ever love.

You writhe from its parting bite,
but it will not kill you.
Since I opted prodigal,
I no longer wish that it would.

John Gascoigne

Taking the Farm Car

There's luck in being alive.
Ravenous for speed,
born determined to drive,

my younger brother would grin
and kid me into another
quick forbidden spin.

Almost standing, he'd peer
over the steering wheel.
Together we changed gear.

Not that gear changes mattered
on the flat and lonely roads
we hungered for. The battered

bonnet shook. Its chrome
spine was a silver arrow
racing away from home.

Windows down, we heard
the shocked fence posts whisper
their indecipherable word,

and the wind gave us its beating,
like a thousand phantom fathers
rushing in and retreating.

We tasted the torn air.
Once, we tasted terror.
Drifting on a rare

bend, the car kissed
railings and bounced off.
Disaster didn't insist,

but I saw the whole world swerve
around us and straighten up.
My brother had kept his nerve.

Shaken, he also kept
the faith. His foot flattened.
Behind us the gravel leapt

and the white dust unravelled
in a long fading cloud,
the ghost of the road we travelled.

Ross Gillett

Australia

Our Earthern dish is seven parts water,
one part China, and a tiny bit japanned.
Its spread of foods is well-presented:
ice sculptures at both poles, and licking-salt
elsewhere. Give me a lever large enough –
a cosmic fork or skewer – and I would take it
to a table: its sherbert fizz of surf,
the creamy ice-cones of its toothy alps,
the spice of islands dotted here and there
like cloves jammed in an onion. Turning
this common dish as slowly as a day, I'd taste
the sweet-and-sour river deltas, the swamps
about its world wide waist, all of which
smell fishy. As do many maps of Tasmania,
most of them in other places: forest fuzz
itchy with green pubic life. Lastly comes
our smaller plate, single and tectonic:
our turf, or lack of it, our baked and gritty
crust, lightly watered, sifter dusted,
and sarcastic with its hints of eucalypt.
Its thousand mile creek tastes too salty,
its muddy waters barely moving, but
moving enough to stir a homesick heart.

Peter Goldsworthy

Petrol

Straight roads, built for driving fast.
You get out of winter in a day.
These paddocks so like thoughts you travel past,
strung out beside your asphalt purpose.

You get out of winter in a day.
Cattle fat as history watch you pass,
strung out and beside your asphalt purpose:
these vast effects of corroded light.

Cattle fat as history watch you pass
with the blank stare of what you don't remember,
corrosive effects of this vast light:
the relics of a gold rush dream.

With the blank stare of what you don't remember,
a pub, a petrol station and a store:
the relics of a gold rush dream;
something so patient you might call it peace.

A pub, a petrol station and a store.
You fill up. In the sudden quiet you hear
something so patient you might call it peace:
crickets, like an electric fence in the grass.

You fill up. In the sudden quiet you hear
these paddocks so like thoughts you travel past:
crickets like an electric fence in the grass
and straight roads, built for driving fast.

Lisa Gorton

The Quick of It

for Graham McDonald, National Folk Festival

Rosellas in the cypress trees
    are feeding upside down
while yellow trucks on demo sites
    cart off the heart of town.
But on this stage two slender girls
    each with a violin,
are fiddling their causerie,
trancing up their sorcery,
loosing the sonar tracery
    that gives our atoms spin.

    The slick of it, the kick of it,
    they're raising up the quick of it,
    there's lightning in their slender bones
    when they lay out the trick of it.

Cameras whirr remotely as
    they close with Saturn's moons,
while economic rationalists
    are churning new tycoons.
But here are girls in jeans who toss
    us curlicues of sound,
their eyes upon some inner thing,
some musical unzippering,
some chaos-theory patterning
    that's lost as it is found.

The lark of it, the Bach of it,
this brim-high watermark of it,
we'll take the light and dark of it
to ride the breathless arc of it

There's ocean freeways drawing whales
    to banquets in the south,
agendas sucking CEOs
    like krill through a humpback's mouth.
But here two heads of nutbrown hair
    confederate with each other
are using fingers and some nous
to make time jump its fence for us.
Lovely the lightning and the fuss
    they toss to one another.

The track of it, the snack of it,
they tuck away the knack of it
and lightning in their slender bones,
gives us the quick wise crack of it.

Alan Gould

Emily's Story

1.
Emily, at four-and-a-half,
is unable to write
anything more than her name

(and she adds extra teeth
to the 'E' until it resembles
a horse-comb), but she has

decided, all the same,
to become the author of a book
which she dictates

to an amanuensis, in terms
like the following: *Emily*
was out walking and she saw

a cockatoo until they flew
up and she played with shampoo.
At our house we saw a cockatoo.

That is a chapter, she declares.
The next one is somewhat shorter:
There was a walking tree.

The tree had little floppy feet.
And then comes: *Someone had two eyes*
and no mouth or arms or hair or watch

or fingers. Each chapter, of course,
has an illustration, drawn
quickly, with an orange pencil:

There was only a yellow girl
with no daddy or mumma
and no brothers or sisters. The tone

is growing dark: *Cyclops*
was angry at pre-school. But
she ends on an uplifting note:

A girl that was beautifuller
than the other girls scribbled on those girls.
She draws golden curls cascading

over the oval skull, and box torso,
of her character, then concludes:
That girl was much more funny, too.

2.
Bitter winter winds. Naked trees.
Shadows like cobwebs or fishing nets

thrown down on the footpath. All day
I stay by the fire, reading some

papers. Emily, at play,
is quiet somewhere else; silence

like a warm cocoon, one might say,
against the cold which hums through wires

outside. Yet it becomes too quiet.
Suspecting the worst, again,

the shampoo emptied on the floor,
perhaps, or a scribbled face

on one of the walls, all there is
when I look is a pile

of clothes, like a suicide's
garments discarded on a beach. Away

down the street the little girl rides
her tricycle, naked as a fish

in the tree-stripping gale,
as if in pursuit of a wish

or of the end to her tale.

Jamie Grant

Joan Eardley in Catterline

The black-faced sheep
are tilted in the storm-light and they face the black-faced
North Sea
on the long decline

of the swollen
pastures. Across all of this, a similar
inertia. The weeds and fence posts come down and hang
above the lane

and we pass underneath
the banks that ooze like a luminous, wrung-out kitchen cloth.
    A barn
opens on a corner
its tunnel

directly out of the gravel
kerb; we slide
by in a car, swishing over mashed cow manure and sliding
    water.
Joan Eardley

came here,
following the reports
on the news, to a place with the worst of
weather, to a cove

that in itself is rough as the jaws of a wrench.
The tight cottages
are fastened to each other and along the headlands
of tight grass; one row on either. Otherwise, there is a pub.

She brought her cancer,
stepped down
into the rattling edges of the bay, with an easel
of lead pipes, it must have been. The storms here are like the
    water's turmoil

in a toilet bowl or
an opened furnace door
of wind and snow. She stood in the sea,
the water ahead higher than her painting board.

We saw this in Aberdeen's
quiet gallery. The sea fell like a weir,
corrugated in black and white. The sky was seasick, a greenish-
    grey, the grey sea
greasy as stone, and its foam

yellow, from the churned-up
shallow floor, or else
there was the release, the transformation, of peach blossom
on black sticks. She broke open

the paint, wound it together, squalled her graffiti
along the water's face, scoured
with blunt spines, tightened everything under a clunky spanner,
    swabbed,
undid at the slice of a trowel, dug

her fingernails in, engrossed. Her subject,
death's approach,
become subject
to her. It was painting as judo.

Or she turned inland, into the passages of the sun –
to an over-ripe
pecked fruit,
which at other times seemed a snivelling, dangled

mucous, and at times had the liquid redness
of an organ
squashed into a jar. The sun, among
the broken panes

of the sticks
and the long grassy skeins,
waning,
was painted as her own,

also, with an urgency occluding distance and time. Bits of
    straw and rope
and grass seeds and bent nails were caught up,
among paint
that she lived in like the mud. Joan Eardley in Catterline at
    home.

I think of someone great,
of Dōgen, in his death poem. 'For fifty years I have hung
the sky with stars; and now I leap through. –
What shattering!'

Robert Gray

The Last Anzac

He has gone out now
further than the little beach
that dreamed his death.

At 103 the years had not condemned –
but wearied him
he no longer believed being sixteen

mattered. He never rehearsed it
in words with anyone
and it never became the fixed bayonet

he eschewed in combat
and that had later rusted into a kind of
forgetfulness. 'Gallipoli

was Gallipoli' his only answer to the
countless questions he'd always been
asked that had no answer. Decades ago

he had left behind the damp hole
he lay in with lice and flies;
enteric fever and bad beef.

His memory had gone on unpaid leave
from that winter of gorse-swept hills
and the ten metres

of blood-soaked ground
they served up at every dawn
after a mean breakfast. And on to

his final morning, he had no allegiances
to history, the war, or anyone:
except himself. And sometimes

through all those years, out of any
connection it seemed, he
would look again on the Aegean Sea

considering it again as he had that
first time, without this past or legend:
so smooth and silky blue; so clear and

cold, so very clear and cold, that
just before you jumped you could look
deep below the boat and see the sand.

Jeff Guess

Sideshow History

Jimmy Sharman's Boxers

wattles have unloosed
their boxing gold

and my hands are
uncured leather

I've fought five rounds
five hard ones, all wins

I've beaten the Greek
seen the Birdsville Maulers

and watched a bit of Sands
now the bees are drinking

from my hands' honey and
I'm itching for Sideshow Street

Jimmy's a bleeding desert pea
and I'm the land's black eye

I'll show him what I can do
but I'll want good money

Jennifer Harrison

Roost

the rain
making little
brown steps
on the roof
henlike
one
following
after
another

then the bees
arrived in the kitchen
clambering
round the weathered
edges of the crack

through the crack
behind each bee
as it climbed
you could see
a wide splinter
of the pearl-grey sky
some
early spring –
sun
behind it

you don't
need money
to imagine
the rain

making rooster-red steps
on the roof
over the kitchen

then
through the iron roof's
russet lace
on
    to the floor below
        water
slowly dripping

            J.S. Harry

Living in M—ls&B—n

I wish I lived in M—ls&B—n
I would be lithe with long legs
and could have red hair and a name like Flame
without anybody laughing.
Whenever I'd get together with Hugh/Roderick/Harrington,
trails of tiny kisses would go just about everywhere
and he would be able
to do extraordinary things to my bust.
Nobody in M—ls&B—n takes it amiss
when things suddenly harden or go soft.
Things open a great deal too,
and buttons go flying all over the place –
in fact the undoing of fastenings and tearing of silks
are the main occupations of the inhabitants
if you don't count the sudden taking-in of breaths.
If I lived in M—ls&B—n
I would have a touch of fire and make his eyes glitter –
mine, of course, would widen, as a heroine's eyes do
when other things harden or open.
M—ls&B—n is a lovely place,
either Majorca or a big hospital or the Outback,
or a small hospital in the Outback.
I can be anyone, but he must have a mouth that can harden
or open, or soften, and is usually claiming mine.
In M—ls&B—n a lot of claiming goes on –
it's the men who are so possessive.
As well, they are thirty-six, tall, dark,
and their eyes have been known to turn into silver slits
under the strain of all that hardening.

If I lived in M—ls&B—n
I would stay delectable forever,
but, with a strongly curved mouth always claiming mine,
and a hand constantly at my fastenings,
perhaps I don't want to live in M—ls&B—n.

Margaret Harvey

Athenian Wolves

The Greeks in the Zappeion feed
A battered old wolf snarling 'Set
Me free to get my own.' In thread-
Bare, dulling coat, I'm much the same,
But better off, having escaped

In middle age from childhood's cage
Of wounds into self-exile, though,
In vaulted concrete cave with tiles,
It's better housed than I among
Low life. Respecting me as one

Of them, their voices drop, as in
My room, or on long cheerless streets
At night, alone, cold and grey, on legs
Thinning under my bulk, I hunt
My family down in packs of poems.

Graeme Hetherington

Triads

after Vincent Buckley

3 things to be expected
  quiet old men
  friendly dogs
  drinkable rain

3 fragile things
  silhouettes in winter
  the patience of a gambler
  empty holes

3 things to be remembered
  a mother's scent
  salt from the sea
  weeds on graves

3 unacceptable things
  lonely babies
  blue bread
  the uncountable dead

3 possible things
  humble leaders
  the wisdom of spiders
  dreams without fear

Matt Hetherington

A Long Swim

Swimming out there
Musculature in ultramarine,
In weed-green sea
You can think 'mackerel'
Till you're blue in the face
But you go like tow rope –
Heavy, frayed, stretched
From pier to pier
From year to year

Entering at the southern one
Mind finned with intent
Crossing crags and sea-grass
Gutters gouged by ebb tides
Rays much wider than beds
Their glide-aways heavenly
Over sands that cloud the hourglass
In light that breaks the light,
Squid invisible, abalone opalescent,
The flood tide your freedom
Its reverse your test of worth

Emerging at the northern one
Your body out of water
Your flesh, on arrival
The underside of flounder,
Each tooth in your head
A little colder, your sense
Of time like coral

Barry Hill

My Father Before Me

Sai Wan War Cemetery, Hong Kong

At noon, no shadow. I am on my knees
Once more before your number and your name.
The usual heat, the usual fretful bees
Fitfully busy as last time I came.

Here you have lain since 1945,
When you, at half the age that I am now,
Were taken from the world of the alive,
Were taken out of time. You should see how

This hillside, since I visited it first,
Has stayed the same. Nothing has happened here.
They trim the sloping lawn and slake its thirst.
Regular wreaths may fade and reappear,

But these are details. High on either side
Waves of apartment blocks roll in so far
And no further, forbidden to collide
By laws that keep the green field where you are,

Along with all these others, sacrosanct.
For once the future is denied fresh ground.
For that much if no more, let God be thanked.
You can't see me or even hear the sound

Of my voice, though it comes out like the cry
You heard from me before you sailed away.
Your wife, my mother, took her turn to die
Not long ago. I don't know what to say —

Except those many years she longed for you
Are over now at last, and now she wears
The same robes of forgetfulness you do.
When the dreams cease, so do the nightmares.

I know you would be angry if I said
I, too, crave peace. Besides, it's not quite so.
Despair will ebb when I leave you for dead
Once more. Once more, as I get up to go,

I look up to the sky, down to the sea,
And hope to see them, while I still draw breath,
The way you saw your photograph of me
The very day you flew to meet your death.

Back at the gate, I turn to face the hill,
Your headstone lost again among the rest.
I have no time to waste, much less to kill.
My life is yours, my curse to be so blessed.

Clive James

Sydney Road Kebab

(The kebab is an ancient Persian form similar to the pantoufle.)

On Sydney Road, kebabs revolve through hungry air,
round the corner from the milk bar, two doors from the pub.
Turbans tangle with tampons in silver glory boxes,
slivers trimmed by skimming knives on Sydney Road.

Fat cylinders of meat lashed to revolving barbecues
choreographed by ratchets, motors, little wheels,
where the traffic is abrasive, grinding slowly to the lights
round the corner from the milk bar, two doors from the pub.

Fat cylinders of meat lashed to a long steel spindle –
cuts of delicious fat, sweetmeat piled on copper plates,
slivers trimmed by skimming knives on Sydney Road –
rolled in a flat bread sheet, beneath a dangling cigarette.

A rotisserie turns Sufi circles through the endless days,
on Sydney Road we feed our flesh with succulence,
with flesh cut from cylinders of meat lashed to
barbecues, as traffic grinds up slowly to the lights.

Traffic aches in smoke-filled eyes of Sydney Road,
saliva on the tongue, fat and salt, then chilli sauce,
rolled in a flat bread sheet, beneath a dangling cigarette –
our hunger hangs on air along the gun-barrel strip.

Fat spits behind the sweaty miles of Sydney Road,
on Sydney Road we feed our flesh with succulence
and your meat must take its turn to face the fire –
rolled in a flat bread sheet, beneath a dangling cigarette.

Sweet street, may your kebabs long revolve in scented air
round the corner from the milk bar, two doors from the pub.

John Jenkins

Bush Versifying

(Female)

.... meet
.... seat
.... display
.... play

.... touch
.... clutch
.... hold
.... mould

.... flirt
.... flit
.... hurt
.... split

.... sorrow
.... mistake
.... tomorrow
.... retake.

(Male)

.... run
.... begun,
.... when up
.... pen-up,
.... fleece
.... release.

.... runt
.... punt –
.... swagger
.... snigger
.... stager
.... wager.

.... tall
.... sprawl
.... sturdy
.... moody
.... heady
.... steady.

.... race
.... apace
.... sweat
.... threat
.... tally
.... rally.

.... quick
.... nick
.... prolong
.... strong –
.... outrun
.... still Gun!

Kathielyn Job

Lachlan Macquarie Inspects Cox's Road

they laid down the road
before him like carpet
(any road being carpet
over those rough house mountains)

he bumped over contour,
can hardly be said
to have travelled it while
road was close-fitting
as hose or corset

carriage-wheels rutted
route like a future
map given imprimatur
of his signature

round about yetholme
he must have beheld
how there were two countries

and for each
inch given in height
a mile was taken
back from horizon

Greg Johns

The Dance

from The Worker Bee Poems

Posture is everything. That and the centrifugal
ecstasies of turning, pivoting on her own

knowledge (it is always a her).
In the depths of longing she is Carmen

Miranda, centre stage, the richest Aristotle
in a Greek wedding's plate-breaking shuffle. A front-row
    Collette

shaking her red skirt, in the bull fight of the *Can Can*.
But there are only two dances, two ways to tell. She is
    forbidden

embellishment. Remembering the complex message
is paramount as she returns from the morning's reconnoitre

to the hive, guided by the avalanche of sun. Like real estate
so much depends on location: the distance of the food she has
    found,

the scent she carries for clues to its trajectory on her filament
    hairs
like a genetic memory of touch. If she doe-see-does in the
    shape

of a heart, the flowers are close. If she sways and shimmies
they are further away. Which is, of course, the sticking point
    between

love and lust. The first,
tumbling into the shape of an empty space that has waited to
    be filled. The second,

a frenetic grab-your-partner bum wiggle
that overflows
    at any old trocadero.

Judy Johnson

Washing Dishes

Traitors
to my rationale, body's
physiology, psyche, my hands

have invented
a new routine
out of discipline learnt
from the handles of a chainsaw.
Weight of factory bricks.
And further back, fibres
of rope aboard a naval ship.
Skinning rabbits
with a pocket knife.

They go down into the warm
sudsy water like a submission
to a new order. Feel about
for the role they once filled,
the position they once owned,
only to be repelled
by the swollen sponge,
hard shape of plates, knives
forks and spoons. The plug
coming out …

I turn on the cold water
to rinse the dishes clean,
and something of who I used to be
washes down the drain.

Martin R. Johnson

Teen Town

for the class of '68

Off North Grand and beside the creek
on a dead-end road lies Teen Town.
We hung out there, biding our time
as the '60s rolled in on the air waves:
Beach Boys, Beatles and the Byrds beat
in our blood like mainlined hormones
till we got every song by heart.
The girls gossiped and we played hoops.

    Holmes flicks a pass behind his back
    to Helme who hits a fade-away jump;
    the Pendergast twins clear the boards;
    and Broph gives an elbow and a bump.

When a .45 was a record
not a gun — that was a .22 —
a .33 was cool, but radio
ruled in a GTO with four
on the floor and a 389.
At sixteen we drove and eighteen was legal
but drinking was a Teen Town taboo,
when girls gossiped and we played hoops.

    Sylvia, Sue, Lonnie and Barb
    had the right look, wore the right garb.
    Songs the end-all, dance the be-all,
    Teen Town revolved around b-ball:

We looked for action on Saturday
night, with a fist-fight as good as
a movie: we knew our roles and
played our parts with a courage born
from fear of failing – that rush
of adrenaline was counterfeit
hate, and friendship the real emotion,
while girls gossiped and we played hoops.

    Holmes flicks a pass behind his back
    to Helme who hits a fade-away jump;
    the Pendergast twins clear the boards;
    and Broph gives an elbow and a bump.

On a rainy day we'd go inside
and try to tease the girls, but girls
know more and decide who's in –
and if you're out you never know why –
so we'd do the dance of not wanting
to dance the Twist, Swim, Pony and Jerk,
Mashed Potato and Locomotion.
Then the girls gossiped and we played hoops.

    Sylvia, Sue, Lonnie and Barb
    had the right look, wore the right garb.
    Songs the end-all, dance the be-all,
    Teen Town revolved around b-ball:

Off North Grand and beside the creek
on a dead-end road lies Teen Town.
The decades pass but the rites are the same,
the only change is in the pronoun.

Paul Kane

Hanoi Girls

Hanoi most sensible of cities —
at night the traffic finally does stop
and a great hush of sleeping
descends: a curtain drawn
down by good spirits
and ghosts about to start work.
Not a sound for kilometres
except a cough deep in a house
a lonely bicycle bell, a word called
out from a dream, a stray bird drunk.
It's dark on the pavement
but the sky glows with smog.
Quiet all night until a rooster crows
sunrise somewhere in the rice fields
behind the rebuilt suburbs
north of the river.
The people who sleep
in the street hammocks are first up
and busy. Everyone's going to work
in an office, school, a sweatshop
or a street stall, hot days get louder
with all the talking it's as if everyone's shouting.
Slow rivers of traffic meander.
Suddenly the girls are there, dozens
then hundreds riding motor scooters
braking gently at the traffic light in Ly Thai To Street
now the traffic flows like waves on a quiet lake.
Cyclo drivers and labourers
might stop for a moment, consider
the day's hot slog is almost worth it,

to see their city's young women growing beautiful
and rich. They remember to be kind to strangers
who try to compare their less cultivated worlds.
What greater joy could there be than to see
Hanoi girls ride motor scooters,
pillion sisters sitting side-saddle.
When the traffic slows they gossip
like tigresses with girls on the other scooters.
Silks and nylon made sure the war
was won by the miniskirt allied with knee-high
leather boots or diaphanous sandals.
Hanoi girls out-glamour the Italians
they fit imitation Gucci so much better
and bring a sense of reticence to leather.
Their mobile phones ring urgently –
lightning strikes Hanoi's holy mountain
friendly rain clouds gather.
Dial an ancestor – mothers and grandmothers
were the bravest women warriors
Vietnam had seen for centuries.
They fought the invaders and lost husbands,
brothers and sons, sisters and daughters.
Everyone lost somebody
when the heartless and stupid ruled America
sent over soldiers and bombers.
The war ended, and lots of grand-daughters,
lots of grandsons came into the world.
Over time the hard times got better
there was food for almost everyone.
The population skyrocketed, as they say, and
Hanoi's grand-daughters grew up and dressed to kill.

Commuting on their scooters they chatter: are love poems
more romantic, more sincere than a gift of flowers,
or just cheaper? there's the wicked past of a Government
Minister who used to be a Saigon pop singer –
too wicked to mention. French football stars
are heading to Vietnam to help improve the local game
ha ha it won't work – the boom in Hanoi's real estate
goes through the roof, So-and-so is starting up
a new business, the new style of Hué cooking
is not so new, those horoscopes in *Sport and Culture*
magazine are so vague to be nearly always right
and the interview with David Beckham
is almost the same as last month's.
To ensure good daughters have everything their mothers
and fathers missed, the sacrifices made are tougher
than to much-loved ancestors –
money to buy a good scooter comes harder
than fake banknotes burnt at an altar.
Hanoi girls pull up at the traffic light
knee-high boots and sheer sandals
rest on the road, mobile phones ring in
a business deal, an old apartment to renovate,
lunch at West Lake. As grandma said,
'when no bombs fall on the polity
it's fine to indulge frivolity'.
Hanoi girls are serious, study and work
their way to the top if that's where life leads.
And by magic, motor scooter and miniskirt
they make the city truly powerful.

S.K. Kelen

Gang-gangs

two Gang-gangs are eating
red berries on a tree in the front yard
they let me stand very close
and ignore me
don't even bother to look at me
I'm interested because
I haven't seen Gang-gangs
here before and as Madonna said
rejection's a big aphrodisiac
so I ask the male
Why the hot pink helmet?
but he still ignores me
intent on snapping off
a tiny bit of tree
I ask His Grand Indifference again
What's with the hot pink helmet?
either he hasn't heard me
or doesn't want to
but SHE stops in mid-squeeze
of a bright red berry
turns into the sun
which ignites the yellow subplot
of her dark pine-cone body
dips her head down my way
and says: *Where's your tail
— all the other kangaroos
have got one?*

David Kelly

All places are distant from Heaven alike

—Robert Burton, *The Anatomy of Melancholy*

Mourning and weeping in this valley of tears
his voice a raincloud through the cane chair-back
where he knelt, head in hands,
and the children bored and silly
under the grandma's Irish Catholic eye.

He was never even tempted
to question the purpose in the will of God.
His torments were the noise his children made,
the bills coming in, the wife he'd thought gentle
setting her face like an enemy.

Home, if anywhere, under the stone roof of his church,
the lovely vertical cold, and in the small time
before the day descended.
Hear, O Lord, the sound of my voice,
hear, O Lord, and have mercy.

Joan Kerr

Loaves and Days

He throws the ball of dough
up above his head. His eyelids
are thick with broken sleep,
his hands white with flour. Lightning
hands. There is a rhythm in this tossing
and catching that is mesmerising,
the unconsciousness of hands
that fling and pluck and fling again.
As if the precious organs of the body
have replaced the dough — a liver
striving for the ceiling, a kidney falling
to an open palm. A heart that is stretched,
kneaded and pumped, then plonked
on the waiting tray. Loaves edging forward
on rollers into a heat that will turn
sourdough golden and cook the crust
of the pumpernickel until it's as hard
as a fist. Loaves running together
like the hours and minutes spent
in the fluorescent glare of Gino's Bakery.
When he watches the last of them
slide away, he only sees bread,
not the tables they'll adorn like cut flowers,
not the man who never cuts an even slice,
or the woman who lifts up the rye
on a breadboard shaped like a bell.

He's had enough of this job, doesn't care
if he never bakes another loaf,
but he loves this moment
when he steps out of the furnace
into the cool darkness of a Petersham street,
runs his hand through his floury hair
and gazes up at the black wires
where the dawn birds line up,
fidgeting like choirboys about to sing.

Andy Kissane

Name

*The name 'Wendy' was invented by a
little girl who died at the age of six.*

Margaret Henley never knew
    Her singular achievement,
So little time there was between
    The birth and the bereavement.

She never knew how wide and far
    Her baby-talk would carry,
The future of the funny name
    She told to J.M. Barrie.

She said her special word and then
    Departed, never knowing
How many little girls would bear
    The name she was bestowing.

She only added to the world
    One unique and harmless touch.
How many glittering careers
    Contributed as much?

Peter Kocan

A Vegetative Life

Beetroot

Cutting you
is pitchforking earth in Silesia.

Under your skin
sombre as last season's nest
lies radical magenta.

Thinking a bright, steaming borscht,
I work in the mud
and the pelting rain.

Asparagus

I smell cut grass –
which is exactly
what you are,
but thicker, more primitive.

Laid on white bread:
green penises draped
in cotton.
The excitement is
in the tip.

Potato

The landlords averted their eyes
when you came up rotten,
collapsed to stinky pulp
in their tenants' fists.

Heavy, solid, a river stone,
now cool and white in my hand –
the newborn smell of spud.

You scattered a generation,
planting Galways and Dublins
in the New World.

Parsnip

You will do
for a witch's nose
or a reverend's
Sunday roast.
Your name is parsimonious
prim and clipped
at the end.
You look so straight
but the devil's in you –
parsnip wine
is the strongest brew
I've ever tasted,
sending the mind
through burning hoops.
Pale digits of the damned,
you go into fire
and come out saved.

Red Onion

Medieval model of the spheres,
gyroscope by Fabergé
You contain infinity –
and make me weep.

Mike Ladd

Distress

She shares her burden –
a small boy with autism,
just now diagnosed.
And my eyes embarrass me
as we speak, until
I must turn my head to hide
my heart. Oh but why,
when I hardly know her, why
do I feel this hurt
at her hurt? I remember
a sage's maxim:
'the feeling of distress is',
he declared, 'the root
of benevolence.' Yes – and
also the reverse:
feelings of benevolence
are the root of our distress.

Andrew Lansdown

The Deep Scattering Layer

Up from the deep scattering layer, where spinner dolphins feed
    on globes and spirals
fleshed with the hunting luminosity of their kind – up through
    the black from which
we crave understanding and poetry, the krill are blowing
    attracted by halogen
lights rigged overhead as snares for squid with oil spills
    around their eyes
and pliable arrowheads on the tapering sleeves of their bodies.
    The krill could be milt
or wake water like aerated protein below the gunwales.
    All night, long lines
set with lures fall and rise, spooling from drums to release
    saltwatersparks
and the severed tentacles of squid that cough and suck
    at tables of blacked-out mesh.
The machinery drones on. A deckhand smokes and stares.
    Behind him, like a stripe
of shadow, strapped and loaded, a .303 Lee Enfield leans
    into the wall. When asked,
he swears that rifle sound is enough to put the frighteners
    on seals that follow
the living lines, though smiles when telling of how
    the blue shark glides
and rolls its eyes as if amused to find itself in a bloodcloud.
    Having said enough
he turns back under the fierce bulbs that burn and light
    the krill, which are now
being culled at the edges by a school of cowanyoung –

bait fish with serrated flanks
and anal spurs, splintering the swell with a sound like gravel
   cast over water.
They divide and reform, divide again as tuna work
   at the speeding silver
plates of their undersides. Ink sheets into the windows.
   Satellite tracking glows
on liquid crystal in the wheelhouse, showing the boat's
   position and depth
of water being harvested. On the floor, in a tray, a frozen roast
   cools the beer slab.
As a floodlit food chain circles stained timber, breaking
   and mending itself,
white shapes surface to flip out onto the deck, where men
   in rubber boots and overalls,
sleep-deprived or drunk, stand at the rails and smoke,
   staring, trying to avoid saying
too much, to themselves or others, in a squall of hard black
   rain.

Anthony Lawrence

A Place

There is a place I like to go
that is behind language

I like to go there and wobble
like a melon on a table

or a spoon that doesn't care
if it is chosen or not

I also like to come back
and slip into 'myself'

like a pair of silk pajamas –
ornamental and cool to touch

Bronwyn Lea

The Planets

Feel good about the planets,
they are your heavenly friends,

set on paths you can only imagine.
Indulge in your life; they do. Go to the party,

achieve a tribal success. Surround yourself
with the arc of their rotation,

devouring as only the truly rotund
in spirit can. Love their magnanimity

and the way they ignore your love. It'll make
you strong. It'll make you look out the window.

Cath Lee

Baudelaire the Bricklayer

after Seamus Heaney's Follower

My father worked like a packhorse.
Striding the grounds he'd survey the site,
Study detailed plans of the house
To be built, his eye a theodolite.

A bloody perfectionist, he'd cock
His head, calculate the gauge, determine
The bond, and drop a plum-line from the top
Of the frame for square, all the while

Looking like a loony with a knotted
Handkerchief for a hat. But he was no fool.
Once a fresh batch of mortar was knocked
Up, he would reach for his tools.

Now his hands moved through air in time
To conduct the scoop and spread of mud,
The lifting and laying and tapping into line
With a hammer, handle or blade

Of the trowel each and every brick
In the walls he called his 'works of art'. Yet I
Failed to see beauty in stacks of bricks
Or a world in a grain of sand, cement or lime.

The building site was a foreign place
Where men spoke another tongue,
Dressed in ridiculous bib-and-brace
Overalls, and whistled songs out of tune.

I never could wear hobnailed boots,
Or take to digging holes with a spade.
'Maybe you'd be better off in a suit,'
He'd say. 'Or learning another trade.'

So I got through the days by reading Baudelaire
And Rimbaud, drinking absinthe, deranging the senses,
Deciding that life is elsewhere
While raking joints and mending fences.

I failed to follow in his footsteps,
Slipped sometimes in my sandshoes
From dodging discarded clinkers, broken batts,
Bricks with double frogs, other nomenclatures.

My father was annoying to work with;
Yapping always, always the verb.
Today his walls still cast a shadow in which
I see a boy awkwardly scrawling his first words.

Ray Liversidge

The Clairvoyant

She leans forward
stroking her left temple
coaxing a lock
then begins to speak
from some place she has opened
within her. A paddock she enters
where the cows graze the past
and chew the cud of the future.
Yes, she milks them
concentrating on the work.
A sincere milkmaid of the future
and whether you drink the milk
she brings is up to you
but you did ask.

Kate Llewellyn

Farmgirl Marries

BRIGHT-EYED SUSIE DROPS BOMBSHELL.
There, at the dining room table, she lets it fall,
news of the decade, they sit in silence
a moment, her mother begins to talk —
SHOCK NEWS DOES NOT GO DOWN WELL.

PARENTS DISAPPROVE.
'Over my dead body,' says Eva as Cliff
clears his throat and removes himself from the table.
They wait for the slam of the door.
SUSIE MAKES MOVE.

GIRL RUNS CRYING FROM MOTHER.
Eva tries to make her see reason:
'It's wrong to marry someone from a different race!'
Susie runs down the road to her brother's place.
SOBBING SUSIE MAKES PHONECALL TO CHINESE LOVER.

'MARRIAGE CAN WAIT TWO YEARS'
says Cliff, extracting a promise
from sobbing Susie. He'll work the miracle yet,
he'll cure his girl of this strange malaise.
NEWS CONFIRMS PARENTS' WORST FEARS.

SUSIE TO MARRY IN DECEMBER.
Can't keep her word. Cliff swears
he'll not attend the wedding. Eva says,
'They're very determined,' and picks up a pen.
CHINESE FIANCE RECEIVES NASTY LETTER.

DETERMINED COUPLE THWART MOTHER'S PLAN.
'Marriage is difficult enough,' writes Eva,
'without your interference,' thinks Susie.
'We'll sign the papers in advance,' says Danny.
FARMGIRL MARRIES CHINAMAN.

Miriam W. Lo

Potato Cutters

They hole up in machinery shed semi-dark
where dust and light are particles
drifting like snowflakes in Christmas baubles,
backlit by sun through a haystack aperture –
a silent-film matinee where actor and audience are one.
They are here to practise the precise wet geometry
of seed potato cutting, a skill hoarded
in cracked brown fingers, aired each year,
flexed and flung at pregnant hessian sacks.
Birth is in those fingers as in a surgeon's,
lifting babe from belly, scimitar knife flying
close to death, squandering no movement
of wrist or eye. They tote their ditty box
of blade and stone, the wife's floor-waxing kneeler
a grudging concession to gibbous spine
and gammy joints, smoko baccy a happier luxury.
I am their slavey – I bring sweet billy tea
and scones in tea towels, watch blurring fingers slow,
jam tins of lime obscure cut flesh, limbs stretch.
Tea looses monosyllables from stiff tongues;
smoko releases a hurry of winged talk,
which dwindles away like spent breeze
to a whisper of whetstone, the settling of bones.
They resume creased silence as if putting on a set
of old work-clothes, fall into dreams
and wonder, at afternoon's end, how all those sacks
were transformed, base metal into gold.

Kathryn Lomer

Oysters in Gravey

a found poem of the fifteenth century

> *'there is no excellent beauty*
> *that hath not some strangeness*
> *in the proportion'*
> —Francis Bacon

Take almondes, and blanche hem
and grinde hem, and draw hem
thorgh a streynour with wyne,

and with gode fressh broth
into gode mylke, and set hit
on the fire and lete boyle;

and cast thereto maces
clowes, sugar, pouder of
ginger, and faire parboyled

onyons mynced; and then take
faire oysters, and parboyle hem
togidre in faire water;

then caste hem thereto, and
let hem boyle togidre
til they ben ynowe cooked;

and serue hem forth
for gode potage.

Yve Louis

Carousel

The music, the giddiness; to remember with a mirror
The locals smiling and fettered
The space undulating
Townsfolk saying you'd come back again

The locals smiling and fettered
You so happy you could have been in orbit
Townsfolk saying you'd come back again
Did it look like we were your stars?

You so happy you could have been in orbit
That dark side, lost to our sight
Did it look like we were your stars?
You ask the question and each reply is the same

That dark side, lost to our sight
A journey, or the end of one
You ask the question and each reply is the same
The planets sure in their step

A journey, or the end of one
The space undulating
The planets sure in their step
The music, the giddiness; to remember with a mirror

Anthony Lynch

Sex at the Poetry Workshop

She came in
as we sat around the table
discussing weaknesses in our poetry.

She told us
one of her girlfriends
hadn't had a man for four years
& was looking for a safe one-night stand.

She told us her friend was coming
to look us over.
We adjusted our appearances
& discussed the importance of metaphors.

Her friend appeared
like a sparkler at a party.
We stood up straight & smiled,
took turns to kiss her hand
as if we were all Romantic Poets.
One of us put his hat back on
So he could doff her.

She wore her hair like a halo
& her shy glances aroused us.
Somebody recited an ee cummings love poem.
The birds started singing like sopranos.
The women went away to discuss us.

She came out of her bedroom & told us
because her friend was Catholic
she had selected the poet
who looked most like Jesus.

The chosen one rose to do his duty.
I tried to wish him luck but he said:
I'd rather stay here writing poetry.
I said: This is a perfect poetry opportunity.
His beard moved as if he was trying to smile.

He left the room as we checked our watches,
shuffled our drafts
listened hard for the softest sound
& returned to the possibilities of language.

Myron Lysenko

Stalingrad Briefing, 1943

The patrols are told to eat snow as they go.
If they do this the enemy marksmen cannot see
the give-away plume of their breath. Smoke

closes over the Volga, awash with bodies entwined
with detritus, riding the dead river, bumping up
against its broken shores. Even colour has been

bombed and shot away; everything has taken on
greyness. The men are grey, their rations are
grey. The light is black and white. The only true

colour left is red. Explosions, blood, a bit
of ribbon. Replacements are told only to carry
their rifles at the ready and step in the footprints

of the men before them. Don't bunch up. Expect
worse than you can imagine. Do not speak.
Stay low and in shadow. Eat snow as you go.

Ian McBryde

The Dissolution of a Fox

For an instant the perfect grass-framed
dead body of a fox, stretched
but as if still running in its sleep,
red-brown perfection of fur,
pointed ears, mouth agape with effort.

Then camera's rapid fast forward
and the eye can scarcely unsort
pieces of this puzzle quickly enough:
as it rushes through unravelling time
animal becomes tufty carcass, insects
like vast columns of removalists
move in. Fox fades to outline, as if
nature has insisted on taking all traces
of its triumph and hoarding it in air.

Shane McCauley

The Up Train

There's no country: Sydney merely thins.
Desperate to get out of town, I lift streets from the soil,
digging for dirt.

To the west, half a rainbow snags clouds. The Egyptians knew
why ibis bend into the waterlogged lanes of Lidcombe Oval
like runners ignoring the gun.

Near Penrith, a hawk flaps angel wings
backwards, black mask round its head, tethered
by a sight line to the need below.

I'm heading where I can hear
crows mourn, watch wag-tails swish their bums
for hours.

The train climbs Linden bush. In the valleys that fall
either side, gum blossom – fluffy as fresh pecorino – sprinkles
whole, wooded ridges. I sit back, happy

as a black cockatoo about to launch its gravity
from a bobbing pine-branch, a baby ape
with a gift pair of wings.

Dennis McDermott

At Scots Presbyterian Church, Kiama

Built of sandstone,
the Presbyterian church
on Terralong Street,
at the edge of Black Beach,
gleams like honeycomb
or wheat, in the late afternoon.

Falling through the fingers of the past,
along the last, shoaling light,
dust drifts to the floor;
like a child passing time
through his fingers
down on the shore.

There seems so much of it
moving through the air – and yet
if it was gathered up
it would amount to little more
than your ashes up the back,
in the memorial brick wall.

I go there guiltily,
for the first time since your death,
to a wall of golden plaques
which look like those on a trophy,
or like the signs beneath
artworks in a gallery.

Each person is like an artist
once their work is complete
and they have left the earth,
or so it seems to me,
as I step
through the crowding dark ...

Startled, I discover your plaque,
and the feeling I have is almost
tangible as the stillbirth
you held in your arms years ago:
you're here with nothing to feel,
and yet you are real.

Squinting now to read,
I see what your life once was:
Devoted wife and friend.
Although you were more than this,
it seems appropriately understated
for, as Hemingway suggested,

whatever has been omitted
from an honest piece of prose
is there just as truly
as if it had been said –
like the milk inside your breast
for the child you never fed.

Am I looking at this honestly?
Then what of the words
I didn't say?
Your plaque seems final, opaque,
this brick wall gives nothing back
but a cold fact:

some words on a plaque in a church
on Terralong Street
by the beach
where a child passed time
through his fingers
with a woman close by, within reach.

Are the natural conditions
which turned sediment to the stone
that went to build this church,
like those that turned the child
to the one
who writes this verse?

Broken as I am,
I want to break it up again
and pass it through my fingers
to my feet at the door;
then feel it blow beyond
the church grounds and the shore

as I step outside the church,
into that growing distance
where you are still alive,
not the writing on the wall,
and I am that child again,
not the one holding this pen.

Stephen McInerney

Alternative Daylights

1.
A beautiful, sexy thing to yawn together
so that bodies sing, each to each
in mute, animal sharing.
Intimate as breakfast,
homely as the memory of early cartoons.
Tigerish too, like a void eye,
an O calling.

2.
Sneezing, old omen when the gods lived in spasms,
is a clean-out for mind as much as nose
as though the idea of no idea
fell out when the brain rattled.
A gentle, joking slap
or a quick glimpse
like a window opened and slammed shut.
Enough to make you see stars
even if the Big Bang goes by unnoticed.

3.
Falling asleep, fainting on demand
is a mental sneeze of the day's dust
and comes over you as slow tingling.
Soft when it comes
like water forgetting its motion.
It's engulfing too, the primordial yawn repeated,
containing an alternative daylight.
Images grow to it thickly like plants.

4.
Orgasm bristles with taboo and consequence
though Sex Ed. likened it to a sneeze.
Like falling asleep and waking at once,
both entry and exit,
a slow-motion flash
that's separate from the merciless attraction,
separate even from bodily art and love.
The quiet moment after two buildings fall together
with nobody hurt, another luminous object, perishable thing.

Graeme Miles

Get the Word

In the beginning was the word
and the word was with God
then a bag snatcher snatched it
laughed and carried it along a laneway
climbed a cyclone fence
pursued by the constabulary
then dropped the word
in an empty playground.

Now the word was with the law
who took it to the station.

But they took their eyes off it.
The word slipped out a window
said itself down a wall
I can I will I am
finding my way to God.

Overhearing was a priest
who dragged it off to seminary
bound it up in leather
shone a torch into its face
said Show the way to God.

The tortured word was honest
but struggled with its bindings
tried to free itself from paper
it was stamped upon
the imprisoned word of God cried

Let me off these pages
I can show the way to love
the one I had with Dad
when he spoke me I spoke him
and when that phrase was in the air
it was the both of us as well.

The priest took the word to council
who took it to committee who slapped it
on the table of a busy bishop
who fenced it from intruders.

But he was knocked clean over
by that scheming snatcher
who took the word and threw it
all over the speaking earth.

Paul Mitchell

My Daughter Reading

My daughter reads in a white hammock,
suspended high in our Cape Lilac.
Its pervasive scent is a sweet mauve smoke
wafting across the yard to where I sit.
It lulls my worry on a gentle breeze,
my anxiety that she might tumble,
tipped from the perch of her green thoughts,
and the day stay indifferent and lovely.
She has chosen an old calico sheet,
slung herself between two sturdy forks,
hauling an encyclopedia after her.
She has constructed this place carefully,
a paradigm of a child's thinking:
it is hung across a clear half-moon
frosting white in the afternoon.
From there she can watch red wattlebirds
sip the indigo evening and goshawks,
white as salt, hunt geckoes in the scrub,
the sea a blue presence in her imaginings.
(She has seen a unicorn from up there.)
Squinting at the emerging flecks of stars,
she queries which one is a planet.
Walking to her I call upwards, asking
the title of the book she ponders.
Tree of Knowledge her smile calls back.
My unease rises with the evening wind.
Later, she climbs down, takes me to safety,
a risk negotiated, a lesson learnt,
moonlight bleaching the shifting sand we tread.

Rod Moran

Banana Villanelle

The world's sexiest fruit is a sterile, seedless mutant ... It lacks the genetic diversity to fight off pests and diseases that are invading the banana plantations of Central America and the smallholdings of Africa and Asia alike.
    —Fred Pearce, *New Scientist*, 18 January 2003

I peel off your skin, tongue my African havana
I love your shape, your bite, your seedless soft
This fruit is a sterile, Cavendish banana

When I am sick, you are heaven-sent manna
I lie back swinging, up high in my loft
I peel off your skin, tongue my African havana

Gros Michel was said to be as sweet as sultana
But was killed off by Panama disease in the fifties
This fruit is a sterile, Cavendish banana

It brings my escape to a tropical cabana
Where dark, lean men labour hard in their croft
I peel off your skin, tongue my African havana

I breathe in your calm, castrato asana
Your gin, sweet food and handcraft qualities
This fruit is a sterile, Cavendish banana

Threatened to extinction by black Sigatoka
I make you part of me, my will and my waft
I peel off your skin, tongue my African havana

I wish us to survive and rejoin in nirvana
Where matter never dies and our sex is oft
I peel off your skin, tongue my African havana
I love you, fruitless Honey, Cavendish banana

Ashlley Morgan-Shae

The Ravenna Job

Up here on the scaffolding I often think
we're working inside the skull
of the man who made this church
with the drum of arcades, niches, vaults
where no shadow can fall straight,
and our mosaics are his Greek dreams,
a rich mist of flora, stars and some angels
soaring to The Lamb; white, simple.

We're in the apse now, finishing
Justinian and his retinue who pause
in their procession, heads in gold,
feet on green, reminding the Ostrogoths,
blonde wreckers from some wolf-
wilderness and their local Latin pals
it is the East which allows their daily sun
courtesy of Byzantium.

This Italy is a cold sour place.
We're restless, aching for the Golden Horn
and raising hell at the Hippodrome
but it's nearly done. I trowel the cement
for the dying priest at the Emperor's side –
Archbishop Maximian, tall, gaunt, hollow-eyed
and sift the boxes of bright tessarae
for his marble chips of white and grey.

The lads suggest we leave him
with a gift. I clip slivers
from a black glass tile while they fuss
about the sight-lines to the lovely girl
in Theodora's troupe with the gown
of cloth-of-gold and the knowing look.
I give him his eyes. He is held fast.
Locked into beauty while these stones shall last.

Kevin Murray

The Cool Green

Money just a means to our ends?
No. We are terms in its logic.
Money is an alien.

Millions eat garbage without it.
Money too can be starved
but we also die for it then
so who is the servant?

Its weakest forms wear retro disguise;
subtly hued engraved portraits
of kings, achievers, women in the Phrygian cap,
poly lecturers who put new states on the map –

but money is never seen nude.
Credit cards, bullion, bare numbers,
electronic, in columnar files
are only expressions of it,
and we are money's genitals.

The more invisible the money
the vaster and swifter its action,
exchanging us for shopping malls,
rewriting us as cities and style.

If I were king, how often
would I come up tails?
Only half the time
really? With all my severed heads?

Our waking dreams feature money everywhere
but in our sleeping dreams
it is strange and rare.

How did money capture life
away from poetry, ideology, religion?
It didn't want our souls.

Les Murray

Guitar Player. Solea

Sacromonte, white
like teeth,
stone
full of mouths;
little hill and
heels upon the wood, stone
upon the light;
slender thighs, brown and shining;
brown and insistent and their secret of white.
Guitar
full of emptiness.
The flash of her teeth
from the full of her lips;
slender thighs, brown and shining
sing deeply her white silence there;
guitar full of emptiness –
o *figura* of wood, bodice of string
which his cunning fingers
can never undo.

      John Augusten Nijjem

September 11th, 2001

Recalled, it may be, in bird shadows
rustling at moon and neon
across the roof-tiles of New York,
these are all fire-people now.
They hung that half hour in limbo
among the false acreage hot-rivets built;
a woman called her lover
and heard his warm voice saying from the sky
that all would soon be well,
till steel columns melted like kite-strings
into blue air, bodies too,
– shadows against the light and heat,
like one who falls upon the sun.

Mark O'Connor

The Hairpin

after the Torinomachi Pilgrimage by Ando Hiroshige

Sunset always makes her think of blood.
The rice-paper screen, blankly portioned out,
is a treaty pushed aside to seize the view.

Through the window's fine crossbars and upright struts
the pilgrimage is a black ant trail in coldest light,
all shadows barred. White Fuji cannot frown.

She and her just-departed guest are guessed
behind the black silk screen through innuendos
over the floor: a wad of tissues, *kumada*-pins to deck her hair.

A cloth and bowl wait on the sill by the scruff-tailed white cat
taut as a knot in his fluffed-out winter fur.
He is the Overseer of the Seven Gods of Happiness

brandished above the procession over the marsh to the shrine.
And the fresh thatch of the two squat huts below
may harbour mice. Rice straw makes his mistress think of gold,

then something left over from autumn – tones and moods,
which stay beyond the law, having no form or edge.
Three lines of wings departing late across

the leached-out sky always blessedly out of reach
will erase themselves to dusk, a code read in the round.
Cat sits tight above the painted panel's Yoshiwara sparrows.

The woman, lazily stretched out naked as non-
existence behind the screen, yawns and fingers a pin
whose tip's too sharp, thinks of a former friend

and a certain point to settle. One breath after
another is pacifying the room. Sunset is the gentlest
despair. Ah! she's made her thumb bleed now.

Jan Owen

Algebra

1.
The way we shuffle pillowtalk
With what our *x*s did

And how they're at a flywire door
Taking back the kid

2.
The way an *x*'s memory dries
Like liquid on the skin

The way they are a souvenir
You can't put in the bin

3.
Two *x*s over cappuccinos
Civilised at last

See how they almost never touch
Too tender from the past

4.
Here now on the courthouse steps
The sky becomes less mean

Though each one's certain they alone
Have had the full dryclean

5.
Two *x*s and their grown-up kids
The nature/nurture ploy

Which one of them can claim the girl?
And which one spoilt the boy?

6.
Although all xs thin like smoke
Their names may be confused

Across a table or in bed
A wrong endearment used

7.
Normally but not always
The in-laws fade because

They seem more certain than the x
Whose fault it really was

8.
When wedding bells are wiped away
The blackboard leaves an image

$2 \times x + 1 + 2$
The algebra of marriage

9.
Some xs drop right off the world
And go to be alone

While others live by email or
The lilting of a phone

10.
It seems that xs never leave
As old friends misaddress

The envelope of their goodwill
Your y is called an x

11.
On seeing xs there are those
You'd cross the road to greet

And those for whom you wouldn't risk
The traffic in the street

12.
Do xs lose the pheromones
That waft between the sexes?

Some moments in a restaurant
Will always be an x's

13.
Two xs in a coffee bar
Give hope for Palestine

Who pays this time, who pays next
A kind of Auld Lang Syne

14.
And finally the day arrives
When neither can agree

On who dropped whom and why – and who's
The dumper or dumpee?

15.
You're probably an x yourself
Statistics say it's so

Some Year 10 sweethearts last until
The fire says who's to go

16.
Deaths are different — often less
Ambiguous — or more

No chances of *rapprochement* and
No shouting at the door

17.
Virgins do not yet have xs
Their time is yet to come

xs add complexity
Intensify the sum

18.
Most equations have an x
Or y and z as well

The Goddess of the Second Chance
Still has us in her spell

Geoff Page

Drama

Uncle Vanya
took me to see
a play
bravo!
bravo! bravo!
he watched me
grow hysterical –
I adored
the long red curtain.

Christine Paice

En Espana

IN SPAIN

I SAW

art	art	art
art	art	art
art	art	art
apartments	a men	artmen
apartments	a men	artmen
apartments	a men	artmen
apartments	apartments	apartments
apartments	apartments	apartments
apartments	apartments	apartments
apartments	apartments	apartments
apartments	apartments	apartments
apartments	apartments	apartments
apartments	apartments	apartments
apartments	apartments	apartments

I BOUGHT

Boots x 2 = sensible
Boots x 1 = frivolous

I ATE TAPAS

YOU ATE TAPAS

Tapas for Two
Two for Tapas

I CLACKED MARACAS, CLICKED CASTANETS
YOU SAID SOMBRERO, EL TORO, FLAMENCO

IN OUR HOTEL YOU ASKED FOR SOAP

AND GOT HAM

IN MY SENSIBLE BOOTS

I walked and I walked and I walked and I walked and I walked and I walked and walked and walked and walked and walked and walked and and walked and walked and walked and walked walked and walked and walked and walked and w a l k e d

WHEN I PUT ON MY FRIVOLOUS BLACK SPANISH
BOOTS – I WEAR MY HOLIDAY

Sheryl Persson

The Ninth Hour

The ninth hour
is here

The ninth hour
makes no sense

The ninth hour
rises up wearily
in a freezing mist.

I have come to a river
of blood and vinegar

I have come to a river
where only pain
keeps its feet

I have come to a bridge
of dissolving bone

I have come to a place
of burning cold

I am trapped in a space
deformed
by my own
leprous fear

have I the strength
to pay suffering its due?

*

There is a calm
that is no cousin
to courage

There is a calm
that sits
like a quivering ape
under the python's
hypnotising eye.

Everything makes you
shiver

The hot wind. The rank river.
The poisonous euphoria.

But it's your shrivelling
flesh
that has the whip hand

Your flesh
has its own tumorous
will

You may think
you have been here
before

You may think
your quicksilver spirit
has your furtive flesh
licked

But darkness
is stronger
than light

The flesh knows best
who'll win line honours
in this fight.

*

The ninth hour
is here

The ninth hour
makes no sense

Don't pray
for a flash flood
delivering miracle
or clarity

During the ninth hour
reason dies of thirst

Your blood stagnates
stale
as a base metal
in your mouth

You dangle
in a cacophony
of retching noise
with no grandiose riffs
of heroism

You will never forget
the foul sound
of the ninth hour.

⋆

I have come to a river
of blood and vinegar

I am here
ninth hour,
I am here
stripped and shivering.

But listen, ninth hour,
listen
and pay heed
to a new sound
in me

I am not here
silent and alone

Do you hear
the fighting hiss
of this geyser
in me?

I stand my ground
in the undaunted spray
and company
of my own words.

Dorothy Porter

To Murder Sleep

I'll dream another worst tonight,
The perfect lines I'll never write,
Some much applauded dumbing-up,
The Gold Experimental Cup,
And prompted by my certainty
Burn Form in its own effigy.

The world is forcing us to show
That relevance may not go slow,
That what might fit is not allowed,
That 'Art To Go' will please the crowd
While self-elected Prophets dwell
In Academia's arc-en-ciel.

Dovetailed with fears of seventy years
A ghostly furniture appears;
It moves with ease from prototype
To fearful dream – its mode is hype,
Panopticon of all that's new,
It gleams in Weekend Interview.

And now it beckons me to sleep
And break the rules I try to keep.
'Remember you were crazy once,
You're still both Neophile and Dunce,
So outperform on death's trapeze
Your competence of enemies.'

Peter Porter

My Wife's Dream

After my funeral
she went exhausted to bed.

Waking next morning
she found me alongside her.

I stirred and yawned.

'Darling, how are you?'
she asked me.

'Oh, OK,' I said,
with my usual

imperturbability,
'just a bit stiff.'

Max Richards

The Day of Singing Bells

Before the world went out for me,
Aware of mercy in the smallest breath
Hurriedly I held you
And wrote the poems that you see.

The urgent song that sweetens death
And the waiting tales we have to tell:
In the winding wilderness of faith
Sing them, sing them well.

May you find that singing tells
And I, when all horizons end,
Whatever heaven may be
Above a day of singing bells.
Did you ring them? You rang them well.

David Rowbotham

This Moon

on the Great Ocean Road from Apollo Bay

Day's end lingers faintly in the belly-flat bay.
Leaving, I drive up, into gum forest
pressed hard and tight into the land.
Road winding, traces the huddle of hills
folded along cliffs that dive
crashing ginger-red ochre into the waves below.
Beyond – the big, big sea.

Out there, on the horizon, a
tangerine full moon rises from raven-shot clouds
in a sky feathered kingfisher blue.
Barely there, its sigh of henna haze is a light veil dropped
in the blackening sky, then lost,
to float orangy wet on ripples close to shore.

If I had just woken
I would think it dawn, and
wonder where sunrise had gone.

Another curve in the road, the sky is black, bereft.
Then behind a harem grille of cloud,
the moon, embarrassed to have risen flushed and unclothed,
reassembles her garb,
cloaks herself in silvery sheath over
shadowy nipples, purpled cleft,
to shine singular, a little haughty, above the turrets.
Beneath, only a pool of talc
on the softened skin of sea.

Two bends more, all light is gone.

Moon, moon –
how lonely the dim road is
without you.

Robyn Rowland

The Family Fig Trees

Seeing them through the mist, on the downslope
from the house, into the wing-lift of swallows,
the fig tree branches rose up like crows-nests,

the ships underground. Or like quattrocento paintings
of the New Testament, each fig tree quite separate
and solid enough to sit on, like a wooden cloud.

When the mist shone flat and silver in the sunlight,
like a thin swamp suspended above the ground,
the fig trees floated in it looking for land.

Each fig split open is the night sky in starburst
down small, ovum and sap, the far-off itching sky,
words I moisten with my mouth like mist.

As a child I sat in the wizened tree, its branches
flattened by my weight, and thought of flat figs
by Cézanne, old varnished figs by the Masters,

these same figs, the pagan, the Biblical mouthfuls,
the erotica of swollen fig, entering the opened fig,
these metaphors which took me past the itch

metaphors stand in for: elsewheres, and sometimes
the lost. I was young, I had not lived, I imagined
the dove returning from dry land, with no branch.

I'd look over to the swamp from my seat in the trees,
the lost banks of the river, wind rafting the surface,
the sky scoured into this water like a metal plate.

The fence posts luxurious with generations of lichen,
and each fence wire rolling mezzotint of stormy skies.
Endless versions. Days passing like drafts of poems.

The fig trees are gone now, dismantled by my brothers.
Too old and too much in the way, old characters
left over from a dream. But I am hurt by what is lost.

Now I sit above another tree, my family, the figurative,
on the table: proof, but only recent, of flattened branches
where the old Sephardic blood-line stops

two layers back: my Jewish grandfather who married out.
When people asked about our name, I might have thought
of figs, opened, like Palestine. But the family denied it.

One tree they took down quietly before we knew of it.
Said we were English, and Spanish married into Welsh.
But close-up, these names are like watermarks.

There's no one to engulf them, or embrace them
now. And now because I cannot claim them right
I call up their music, and if I cannot hear it quite

there's a sweetness I can taste above the branches
in my chest, in *this* tree, this wooden cloud of names:
Mordecai and Sarah. Noah and Ruth. Shalom.

Philip Salom

Saxophone in a Pawnbroker's Window

Lost days when cavernous notes
reverberated seismically into the night,
or rose like an exotic flower,
wild and potent, a soloist's territory,
far from eyes locked
on the instrument's price.

The neighbours wished for him
and his gleaming saxophone, a gig,
or frozen keys, glad to miss
the magic of his fingertips.

Now it's a mirror for peering
shoppers, madly skewed;
and at a stretch along its tube,
the street curves weirdly
where the saxophonist
lost control of the one bright
ally with any value –
a beacon among cold rings
and trinkets for him to brave
the crazy way back
to meet his own reflection,
just in time, and get the music out.

Andrew Sant

Looking for Ancestors in Limerick

Take a myth with you, they said.
I took memories of my grandmother and forgot
Death certificates, marriage documents — there was no
Birth certificate. I took myself.
My grandmother had a voice like musical bottles
And a temper like my daughter. She swore
In the language of petulance in her old years.
Younger, I can believe she equalled
The fabled flood of '93
Or the 1954 cyclone. My grandfather
Would go outside and feed the chooks.
'Buy her a bonnet when she's like that,'
was his advice when I married. My grandmother
was radiant as rosebushes after the storm.
I took memories.

Her mother died in childbirth and Connor,
Her dad, took a ship to Philadelphia, with promises.
She was raised by her grandmother. Widowed,
The old one carted the tribe out to Australia
To a married daughter. My grandmother was a child
When the old woman died. They were out walking.

Absences became part of her upbringing.
She was small as a hand-held gun and she
Could be soft as the first hush of a bushfire.
I feared and loved her and her stories were fragrant
As new-dug earth in the back paddock.
She wore her hair short. When bobbed hair
Became the style she led the fashion.

She was never a follower. She was the one
Who hoarded an ominous Celtic legacy.

I arrived at the village, Broadford, with an accent
Now recognised in film and TV. No Aussie
Tie pin or koala souvenir but my stance
Was a gumtree in that green bog land,
'And what will you find?' my host asked, kindly.

One never expects recognition
But I was greeted by likenesses. The wife of my host
Exclaimed, 'Those hands –
They are your own father. And the shape of the head,
It is himself!' They helped me track down
The long missing birth certificate
And the Enright and Kiley gravestones.

But my grandmother had never told me
This village was the site of the last Bardic School
Under O'Bruadair. That Irish Bard
Seems to be known now only for his Curse Poems.
Reading them I cannot avoid catching the lilt
And the vehemence, the exile and the anger
I had thought uniquely that of my grandmother.
I took a myth back with me. My senses
Have already been infected.

Thomas Shapcott

Wine

I was in my late teens when I met you,
Though I'd seen you at the edge of things before.

You were Claret then, in casual dress
In a two-quart flagon.
No one drank you in full view.
You grew old on the cool-room's topmost shelf
Beside your paler twin, dry Sherry, kept
For snifters and desserts.
Children never knew what you were for.

You put on fancy dress in cocktail bars and parlour escritoires
In houses of my relatives: fruit liqueurs' neon tones
In Bauhaus and Art Deco bottles: apple, peach and apricot.
The cherry's tart reminder of the soul of fruit apart,
You smacked of medicine, not things contrived for joy.
Sticky drinks were not what poets thought of
In their wine-lists in old times.

I met you next at parties in the days when I was poor:
The young rough red that washed down baked tomatoes,
Homemade bread and chat in houses with no furniture,
Or flats above bordellos, where you stained the landlords' floors.

You moved up, to inhabit slender bottles, tried your French
On those who dreamed of foreign travel, went to parties
And, in Spanish-labelled bottles, you made frequent guest
    appearances
In restaurants with lovers who supposed that that fine villa
In the picture on the label was your home.
Candles lit up more than that illusion.

I passed your local home on bitter mornings
As I rode a motorcycle from the mountains to the city:
Vines leaned heavy on their trellises in mist.

I drank you rough and fortified, in smoky rooms
Where jazz bands played while people lost their thought
Or gathered courage to accost attractive strangers,

And in thin historic bars I met your devotees
Who spoke of you with reverence, took you plainwrapped
To their plein air homes in parks.

I saw you handed round at gallery shows
Where conversation flowed like money,
And you did not count for much, but hastened sales.

Once, your resin flavour moored a café outside time,
And the afternoon that followed in a borrowed room
Returns each time you're poured.

Michael Sharkey

Belief in Ghosts

'Almost 7000 people disappear every year in the area covered by the (London) Metropolitan Police Service alone ...'
                    —The Times, 10 July 2000

I have not forgotten you
or forgiven you for disappearing.
I've seen your last hours reduced
to four and a half minutes in a TV segment,
and the questions it asked were reflections
shivering in a puddle. You have been taken
from me, and this knowledge treads lightly
on the floorboards of my memory.
Fear approached from behind and placed its hands
over your eyes and mouth and any protests
were swallowed like the gasps
of someone drowning, someone swept away.
The shutter to a camera's eye closes
like the lock to a darkened room
and you are captured forever on a faded poster
in a police station. You are my grief, frozen.
I make a composite of your face
from the features of everyone I look at.
Your absence hangs from a spider's web,
but I have no bones or ashes.
Significant dates drift away, just mantras
repeated with failing faith, petals falling
one by one from a bouquet.

Yet I survived all this and still seek you out,
believe that I can find clues
which will lead me out of this maze
which runs from hope at one end
to whatever else awaits at the other.

Shen

Suburban Confidential

The pickpockets at Randwick called their business Skims.
They had Fly, Gloves, and Legman instead of Christian names.
They said wads were Crops and talk was Mail.
Watches and bracelets were Tin.

Jockeys whip with a little oar. But *they*
called Whipping the fingering for black wallets
tucked like the skin of the heart.
How do you do it? I asked. 'Practice. Practice.'

I was crouched in walk-socks, underfoot of the people,
scouring for winnings among discarded slips.
There they stood in their tracksuits, Love-Hate on their
    knuckles,
'We call you Periscope,' they said,
'The way you're up-down in the Herd.'

From the um-pah-pah rotunda I watched
their pincer-move below: Fly sauntered
anti-clockwise to the crowd and threaded
his arm in-out of the Joe.

Gloves took the pass in a newspaper mitt
and snuck it to Legman who squeezed into the sun
where a bugle called for Horsemen of the Optimists
to canter to the barrier please.

Practice. Practice – I tried it at home.
In my father's wardrobe there were seven pinstriped suits.
I play-picked their pockets till the hangers
didn't swing fanning his smell's creamy lotions.

At my mother's end there were purses with crossed fingers:
I pried in their bladders with a soft unspring.
She had hair plaits and earrings like clip-on oysters,
pearl handfuls and chainy tangles.

I wore them with lipstick at her sit-down mirror,
and fell in love with my boy-woman skin.
When bored with wrapping her scarves into turbans
I kissed the glass in puckered mists

and searched the drawers for something confidential,
a secret compartment I could spy in.
Of course there was no such thing,
no glamorous code-books,

no false walls with diamonds.
Handkerchiefs and socks covered what was private:
a book of sex acts called *Danish Passions*,
an opened pack of condoms.

Craig Sherborne

Dreams of Dead Poets

Time was, I would have died for such adulation,
    given up a decade for a day of it.
My volumes dance in all the literate bookshops,
    pupils sift my enjambments for a sign,
my symbols scatter like dust about the land
    and all the quarterly reviewers now
drop my old name as if it were a chant.
    In short, I am a poet on the crest of fame
every anthology's incomplete without,
    my statue looms erect in pantheons
and I've inspired a thousand lesser gods.

Yet as I sit and scan the other side
    a horrible despair encircles me.
I've learnt about the suffering of the dead –
    much blacker than the half-blind pangs of life.
I am objective, but not yet detached
    enough from that poor ego I inhabited
to stay unmoved by seeing what I see.
    The stuff's no good!
The lines I sweated over mock me now;
    those random clusters of inspired gloss
stand like a sentence, and my cleverness,
    that self-reflecting eloquent facade,
haunts immortality from the halls of time.
    I can see through it all –
I was no poet: yet I could have been,
    perhaps, perhaps, if I had stopped to hear
that which was truly happening within.

And oh, the verses I could *now* create
from these half-listened-to, half-done designs!
    I could rewrite my whole inheritance –
or most of it: there is the poem or two …

I curse this clarity!
    Soon it may scarcely matter. But now I'm helled,
like a poet at night, in one last desperate quest:
    I must find Milton, Botticelli, Bach.
There are some urgent things I need to know.

Alex Skovron

The Deep End of the Pond

Curious to see how deep
was the pond
I plunged my hand
into the deepest end –
but quickly withdrew
when I felt the cold
encircle my arm like an icy clamp.

Trying again, more cautious,
I anticipated
the grasp of darkness and cold –
as my fingers probed
the depths for stones and slime
and my arm descended
lower and lower.

Nothing. Nothing to feel
and discover.
The pond was deeper
at its deepest end
than I'd ever imagined
while standing at its edge
in daylight or in darkness.

Edging away from
the untouchable bottom –
towards lily pads and duckweed
at the other end,
my fingers encountered
stones, mud, tubular stems
snaking to the pond's perimeter.

An inexpressible joy
passed through me
as flesh made contact
with fibrous matter –
feeling an affinity
with what I understood
and not what had evaded me.

I stood up, stepped back
and took measure
of what I'd just done –
seeing a fish surface
from the deepest end
and turn on its side
like a knife waiting in the water.

Peter Skrzynecki

Decision

Strolled into the office, of
reincarnation, though still
undecided, of my desired formation,

they tempted me almost, to sign up
as a whale, but I've seen many
beached, and rescue attempts fail,

and though I've held dreams, in the freedom
of birds, I've also seen cages of parrots
with words,

so I signed up for some more, of what
I've already had, for only a human
can see what is sad.

Andrew Slattery

Kidding Myself in Kuta, Bali: A Pantoum

They've hired too many actors for the scene
The piles of bodies really are a laugh
The wounds are so extreme that they're obscene
With limbs ripped off and bodies cut in half

The piles of bodies really are a laugh
The blood however excellently done
With limbs ripped off and bodies cut in half
While all around the crimson rivers run

The blood however excellently done
Confused? Concussed? A little drunk perhaps
While all around the crimson rivers run
I am the one in shock who laughs and claps

Confused? Concussed? A little drunk perhaps
At last it dawns, there is no camera crew
I am the one in shock who laughs and claps
Hawaiian shirt with blood now streaming through

At last it dawns, there is no camera crew
A laugh chokes in my throat, I'm sobbing now
Hawaiian shirt with blood now streaming through
A man in white sticks something on my brow

A laugh chokes in my throat, I'm sobbing now
The frantic search for living victims starts
A man in white sticks something on my brow
He smiles and whispers sorry and departs

The frantic search for living victims starts
A second man comes close, and shakes his head
He smiles and whispers sorry and departs
I can't accept I'm very nearly dead

A second man comes close, and shakes his head
I do not want to face my life's conclusion
I can't accept I'm very nearly dead
It's just a film: my final self-delusion

I do not want to face my life's conclusion
They've hired too many actors for the scene
It's just a film: my final self-delusion
The wounds are so extreme that they're obscene

Alan Smith

Friends and Ancestors

Fresh from reading sharp, kind Sydney Smith;
another horror heads the midday news,
another massacre of innocents.
What can I do? Just turn the set straight off?

In 1823 Sydney exploded:
'Do not drag me into another war.
I am sorry for the Greeks and for the Spaniards,
I deplore the fate now of the Jews.
Baghdad oppressed, Tibet not comfortable
and trouble brewing in the Sandwich Islands.
Am I to fight for all these different people?'

He showed friends how to manage day by day:
'Find room for laughter. Try to do no harm.
Take short views of life. Beware of poetry.
Spend more time out in the open air ...'

There is a corner near the backyard steps
still frequented by the winter sun
and by my neighbour's biscuit labrador.

Thinking of Sydney Smith and all his friends,
perhaps I'll count him as an ancestor.

Vivian Smith

Crow Committee and Raven Review Board

On every road you travel, they are there
a delegation from the one big government
picking through the facts like a royal commission
reading the entrails as soothsayers do.
These are the beaks who can't be bribed
whose gravitas cannot be shrugged aside
like a mournful garment only worn sometimes
to hide the ordinary mortal underneath.
No: here is principle personified
pacing the corridors of power like metronomes
their gait ponderous, delicate, but never undignified.
Hereditary chamberlains born to serve,
their life's mission bred in them bone deep
and extruding outwards into stiff formality
crisp practicality, never cruel nor compassionate,
simply elegantly factual and dispassionate.
On every road you travel, you will see them
a conference convened at the scene of the crime
a coronial inquiry examining the evidence
an independent committee investigating corruption.
Here is such plain uncomplicated probity
the whole process transparent, conducted publicly,
no decision of theirs is ever disputed,
no conclusions they make can be refuted.

Edith Speers

Rosellas

It seems your being eight happens
the moment you stand still enough
for wild rosellas to descend
and wrap you in their richly red,
blue cape. Unlike your dress-ups,
they're autonomous. You cannot put
them on. And so your ardent wish
becomes the will to hold birdseed
in steady, aching arms. Only
when you've embodied their desire
do you receive the robes you're
waiting for. So, as the cliché goes,
it's hard to say if you're controlled
or you control the birds. Neither,
and both. Your being meets theirs with
the poise of flying buttresses.
Like left and right hands learn to meet
when building card houses. One bird
lands on your head, grasps forcefully,
takes off to liberate the lightness
there when you first sense yourself in
equilibrium with what you're not.

Sue Stanford

The Knitting Woman

Your hands closing on shadows
there you stand
looking into your self
as if into a cup
eyes vacant or aghast
emptied as if by sudden death.
Such terrible sadness.

Patience comes before love.
Time is God's hands, and
God is the clock of our lives.
But is this good news as you lie
lonely in your bed
spinning jumpers of light
for handsome men?

Kathleen Stewart

The King of Prussia Reveals

'King George III of England addressed an oak tree in Windsor Park as the King of Prussia — and was subsequently treated as insane. But the King of Prussia reveals that he really is an oak tree.'

Poor George.
I was that tree
still am.
I chose to be an oak —
oaks have such a long life span
hundreds of years in fact.
I would not want to live
for hundreds of years as a human being though
      that would mean hundreds of years of wars.

Having a Prussian boyhood —
and a Royal one at that
I was taught that
man's greatest delight is
'War.'
That is why
I became a tree.

To begin with
standing in one place was difficult
but I found that
trees are content
to move slowly
which gives us time to think.

After a hundred years or so
I came to realise that
being constantly on the move
is a curse to mankind.
My slow roots touch stones
caress bones
and lie on the truth of things,

There must be others who like me
have become
a tree.

In time I shall hear of them.

Maurice Strandgard

Journey

The door slides shut with a hiss and it seems we're moving out
    falteringly at first, the brick
    flats tilting then
    reluctantly shifting
aside. We're starting a long journey with half the plot,

some of the story, nothing to worry about and hardly a clue.
    Now a canal's rotating slowly,
    now a sodden paddock, starring
    a wrestling girl and boy.
All gone; we've had quite enough and we're shooting through.

It's hooroo to the broken mirrors and the scraps of sky
    glaring from the wet turf,
    the torn panties,
    grass stains; turn
your back and be rid of the lot of it, say goodbye.

Somewhere long ago you hunted among the chatter
    clutching a damp hand,
    frightened of appetites,
    bold, shaking, wondering
why she wanted you so much, and what was the matter.

And now she's disappeared, or what's worse, turned into just
    another bothered mum. Back
    there in the twilight
    then, she was a pink
breathless angel, all clumsy enthusiasm and lust.

They hope for more, they all want something mysterious,
    the heartbreak girls, the
    lost lads, it's no
    thanks to the bread of life
but give them a piece of cake and they go delirious,

wanting the sun to dazzle and stand still forever,
    youth to ripen, passion
    to flicker and flash,
    every cheating
kiss a puzzle, true love a paradox and a fever.

And what are you doing here? Do you deserve it?
    Dodging the blades, weaving
    between the wheels and not
    getting the chop?
You're hardly the handsome dandy after all, more the nervous

middle-aged college visitor bewildered at tea,
    ashamed of his tie:
    the wrong badge,
    prickly hedge, life
a locked book and an idiot rampant in a tree

wondering what the fuss was about at the front of the hall:
    the shriek, the slap,
    the shattered glass, the
    burst of clapping,
the stock market crash and the shock declaration of war.

And we seem to be rattling out of control along the track
   that clatters into the
   country, turns a bend,
   and vanishes into
the forest, into the waiting shadows, into the dark.

John Tranter

A Steam-driven Computer

Proud Lord George Byron
needled his generation
limping to sundry boudoirs
writing measured verse
revelling in languid despair
pen and penis his passions

Boring his way through
bevies of effete belles
fascinated by his verse
and languid good looks, but
with his lawful, ill-used wife
begat his greatest work

Ann Byron Lovelace had
a greater claim to genius
with a mathematical mind
surpassing father George
comprehended Babbage
and his difference engine

Without spouse Lovelace
a spendthrift, gambling fop
she could have made
the world's first computer
and properly programmed it
driving it with steam

And good Queen Victoria
Prince Albert duly consorting
may have witnessed
a computer revolution
and frock-coated stellarnauts
a-landing on the moon.

Walter Vivian

king

leaving Bris Vegas
1a.m., Eastern Standard Time
my butt 10 inches off the bitumen
                      travelling at 100 klicks an hour
                                          feet up on the dash
acting every bit like I think an immortal would
                                      maybe?

for now though
            this is living,
                    sun roof open
jet-stream preening the cigarette composites off my white suede muse,
Georgia's in her own world
            by my side
                    modelling a steering wheel
                          and a white straw cowboy hat,
she's wiggling to the woofers
                  this is living
ejected from the smoke-infested nightclubs
            Kylie Minogue is taking us both home tonight
So I should *be so lucky!*

yet, all I can think about is the King;
                        I THINK,
                        THEREFORE I AM ...
heaven is framed in the sun roof,
and as I look up and salute
                  the stars wink back
                        across Elvis' rhinestone ceiling

                              Samuel Wagan Watson

Boleyn, Tourist

Dear, stinking city, such a hive
of shoulder-wrenching power play
                        and loose heads,
so I won the endgame, after all,
and the silken skirts of my daughter
are flaring out across a chequered kingdom.

Oh yes,
           the city is pure extension:
it is all milk, it grows mother-of-pearl,
blazing water and eye-watering light
over to the dock-pocked shore
and cruel Tower, softened like china-clay.

                The self knows no bounds at all,
                connected to violent eternity
                by tranquil passages
                of some disembodied pigment.

                But London throbs with morning.

Illumination carries me away
ripping a mortal grid apart, the sometime flesh,
and thus dunking poor old self
in the silken texture
of never dying at all, being one of the gods
in the long, dazzled run.

                            Chris Wallace-Crabbe

Mr Waterfeet

I am listening to my sons
in the other room.
They are playing,
fishing for Sneaker-Head Sharks,
hand chopping them in frenzy,
killing them joyfully,
the eldest running off
a full commentary,
the youngest obeys direction,
'Chop! Chop! Chop!',
shoes clumping to the floor,
'14!, 15!, 16 now!'
An old persona,
Mr Waterfeet,
surfaces.
He is the unheard narrator,
the whisperer of story,
their ancestor.

'Has the big wave come yet?'

'I'm looking in the air.'

'I saw a glow.'

'Now you're the water!'

Meredith Wattison

Ballade for Alan Gould

What's in a name?
            —Alan Shakespeare

Dear Alan, with benignest aims
(you're telling me indeed *What's in …*)
I give you not immodest claims,
nor self promotion's wincing din
(non-Alans need to bear this, grin,
unless you're one you'll never know)
our king of names demands it so:
with simple maximised endeavour
watch my ballade's blazon flow:
We Alans always stick together.

No minnows in the name big pond:
Turing, Lomax, Greenspan, Fels,
even our black sheep Jones and Bond;
the world takes note and something jells:
there's that big-heartedness which tells
we're democratic by the gallons.
just reinvent yourselves as Alans,
give the past a mighty sever
Ahmed, Boris, tip the balance,
join the name that sticks together!

Near holy writ, you know it pal,
like in a movie starring Ladd
that sheer delight in being Al:
the word gets out how, man, we're baaaaad!
Chicks just swarm to Alan's pad.

Or we're a Test team led by Border
who'll willingly obey this order
(seize the willow, whack the leather!)
in mateship pure (there's little broader)
we Alans always stick together.

Claudes make way! Move over Jasons!
We lay it wide and lay it thick.
You'd think we were a mob of masons
to see backscratching do the trick:
when poesy meets biopic
who'll play the Curnows, Ginsbergs, Tates?
Why Messrs Alda, Rickman, Bates.
(Met any poet first name Trevor?
His lonely, untuned, tin ear grates.)
Muses and Alans stick together.

Piss off Con 'n' Don 'n' Ron,
the world has not seen lesser beaux.
Like Monsieur ('ow you say?) Delon,
there's one way for a name to go:
ditch that Edgar, Mr Poe,
join *my* friends Alans Wayman, Murphy:
airborne, waterlogged or earthy
their word is law to end of tether.
Backsliders? Hardly! What a furphy,
both they and us will stick together!

Pettersson, Musgrave, Jeans and Price
all helped to build the Alan pie.
For kudos, though, please give that twice
since be it known that you and I
can only hold up half the sky,

and needing those who'll share our vistas
– since there's a Ms for all the misters
(Kyle has Kylie, Heath has Heather)
four simple words adorn our sisters:
Alannahs always stick together!

And since our name's the sweetest fate
here be our slogan, better, motto
If he's an Alan he's a mate.
(Who'd ever be a Merv or Otto?)
Like endless First Division Lotto
our deal is trumps, our crown is jewelled.
And furthermore all gods have ruled:
from big bang to the twelfth of never
(no need to tell *you* Brother Gould)
we Alans always stick together.

From yoohoo unto toodle-oo
your days are over Jean-Paul, Lou,
our cause is a when not whether.
One l, two ls, a, e, u
(oh band of brothers! happy few!)
we Al(l)a(e)(u)ns always stick together.

Alan Wearne

What the Pumpkin Knows

What is it they say in Sierra Leone?
– There is nothing about the inside
of the pumpkin
that the knife doesn't know.
Nothing about the knife
that the pumpkin
can't forget.

Every evening, so routine,
another small colloquial crime.
Another curfewed massacre.
And then the cleaning up.
The questions in the news;
and her eyes
on screen.

The journo asks
Which is worse: guns or planes?

Her eyes
on screen. Not mine.
Not my son.
My house, my yard
not mine;
my son, not mine.

And what is it they say in Sierra Leone?
'For a funeral, any kind of crying will do.'

Jen Webb

Mrs Jackson

It's as if someone has drilled a hole in her head
and drained the knowledge out

Masters in Education, sixty years of tertiary teaching
six textbooks on Pitman shorthand

(a female figure stencilled on the toilet door
is the only abbreviation she needs now)

her husband dead for thirty years
'An Irishman, filled with jokes. No

no children; although we tried quite hard, he, he!
No, it was great disappointment to us, still

that's the way things are.'
She gets lost trying to find her bed

walks with her palms on her hips
'… to keep my balance …'

prefers the company of women
although I persist

and so she talks to me, hands me a gift
I cannot receive enough of.

John West

Voyage

for Clifford and Catherine Overton

The man who suddenly saw his five-year-old daughter
ascending the ski-lift alone and unbuckled
was not Dedalus, nor she Icarus.

She passed him as she passed the sun.
He could not tear his eyes away, and prayed
she wouldn't see him; one glimpse of his fear

might bring her tumbling sixty feet.
So he stood, a scarecrow of distraction on the snow
and dream-like she sailed up through blind-white cloud.

Petra White

Comic Actor

for Howard Stanley

His face is a yard of clever dogs,
rushing about, happy to follow
intricate instructions.

Beautiful ensemble work, nothing
this well-trained team can't do.
They chase each comedic nuance
to its joke, herd confusion into certainty
and out, track and flush conflicting emotions,
bring down the bird of happiness and carry it
loyally in a soft mouth
to lay before tragedy's door.

Applause. The panting actor bows.

Dawn lights an empty yard, a master
blank a-blanket in the solemn joy
of sleep, the working dog's reward.

Lauren Williams

Golden Hands

she lives across the road from the corn
field, her house loosely penned
by animal runs and rooms her husband
has built on over years of weekends

when his children visit
he cuts down homemade salami from
the rafters of one of these rooms
a froth of blue mould curves along its seam

when he's not home she sometimes
takes off her scarf and dances with the turkeys,
lifting feet in 'levi' mules, shaking
down a rain of grain and lettuce ends

she says these are her golden hands
the nails have blackened cracks down their length
she warms them in turkey blood, dishwater, spinach soup

she sits with her feet up on the bench and chews
the dry dark orange corn, her golden teeth

Morgan Yasbincek

Far and Near

in australia
i am as far from any australians
as china is from australia

and i am as near them
as a cloud
near the sky

Ouyang Yu

Publication Details

Jordie Albiston's 'Collectables' appeared in *The Fall*, White Crane Press, 2003.

Lucy Alexander's 'Trajectories' appeared in *Feathered Tongues*, Five Islands Press, 2004.

Judith Beveridge's 'The Dice-Player' appeared in *Wolf Notes*, Giramondo, 2003.

Elizabeth Blackmore's 'Dog Bite' appeared in *Blue Dog*, Vol. 2 (3), June 2003.

Anna Buck's 'Two Out of Ten' appeared in *Quadrant*, May 2004.

Joanne Burns' 'salt' appeared in *footnotes of a hammock*, Five Islands Press, 2004.

William Carney's 'Notice' appeared in *Quadrant*, December 2003.

Alan Carvosso's 'On Wings of Song' appeared in *Meanjin*, Vol. 63 (1), 2004.

Gary Catalano's 'River Song' appeared as an epigraph to a catalogue of paintings, *Euan Heng: Elsewhere*, Australian Galleries, 2004.

Sherryl Clark's 'Waitress' appeared in *Said the Rat!: Writers at the Water Rat*, Black Pepper, 2003.

William C. Clarke's 'At the Pantheon' appeared in *A Momentary Stay*, Pandanus Books, 2003.

Hal Colebatch's 'Red-head with Phosphorus' appeared in *Quadrant*, January–February 2004.

Jennifer Compton's 'Wave to the Queen' appeared in *Parker & Quink*, Ginninderra Press, 2004.

Gregory Constantine's 'The Book' appeared in *Quadrant*, December 2003.

Meg Courtney's 'Sinking Ship' appeared in *Quadrant*, October 2003.

M.T.C. Cronin's 'The Law of Kindness' appeared in *Poems Niederngasse*, Switzerland.

Luke Davies' 'Supple' appeared in *Totem*, Allen & Unwin, 2004.

Bruce Dawe's 'Hang in There, Boy' appeared in *The Headlong Traffic: A Collection of Poems and Prose 1997 to 2002*, Longman, 2003.

Michelle Dicinoski's 'Lexicon' appeared in *The Weekend Australian*, 28–29 August 2004.

Jane Downing's 'A True History' appeared in *Quadrant*, April 2003.

Stephen Edgar's 'Entropy Blues' appeared in *Lost in the Foreground*, Duffy & Snellgrove, 2003.

Suzanne Edgar's 'The Loneliness of Salt' appeared in *Quadrant*, September 2004.

Russell Erwin's 'The Cruel Prayer' appeared in *Quadrant*, May 2004.

Steve Evan's 'Left' appeared in *Taking Shape*, Five Islands Press, 2004.

Diane Fahey's 'Macaws' appeared in *The Age*.

Johanna Featherstone's 'Tokyo Metro' appeared in *Quadrant*, June 2004.

Barbara Fisher's 'Flight into Egypt' appeared in *Quadrant*, June 2003.

Carolyn Fisher's 'Potato Country' appeared in *Quadrant*, October 2003.

William Fleming's 'Le temps a laissié son manteau' appeared in *Quadrant*.

Lesley Fowler's 'Reviewing' appeared in *Said the Rat!: Writers at the Water Rat*, Black Pepper, 2003.

Adrea Fox's 'Red Felt Hat' appeared in *Said the Rat!: Writers at the Water Rat*, Black Pepper, 2003.

Jean Frances's 'Homage to Satie' appeared in *Quadrant*, May 2004.

Katherine Gallagher's 'At Delphi' appeared in *The Weekend Australian*, 8–9 November 2003.

Ross Gillett's 'Taking the Farm Car' appeared in *Quadrant*, November 2003.

Jeff Guess's 'The Last Anzac' appeared in *Winter Grace*, Five Islands Press, 2004.

J.S. Harry's 'Roost' appeared in *Southerly*, Vol. 63 (2).

Margaret Harvey's 'Living in M—ls&B—n' appeared in *Quadrant*, March 2004.

Graeme Hetherington's 'Athenian Wolves' appeared in *Quadrant*, June 2004.

Matt Hetherington's 'Triads' appeared in *Surface*, Precious Press, 2004.

Clive James' 'My Father Before Me' appeared in *The Times Literary Supplement*.

John Jenkin's 'Sydney Road Kebab' appeared in *Dark River*, Five Islands Press, 2003.

Kathielyn Job's 'Bush Versifying (Male)' appeared in *Ask the Rain*, Poets Union Inc. Anthology, 2004. 'Bush Versifying (Female)' appeared in *Quadrant*, September 2001.

Greg Johns' 'Lachlan Macquarie Inspects Cox's Road' appeared in *Quadrant*, June 2003.

Judy Johnson's 'The Dance' appeared in *Blue Dog*, Vol. 2 (3), June 2003.

Martin R. Johnson's 'Washing Dishes' appeared in *The Earth Tree*, Five Islands Press, 2004.

David Kelly's 'Gang-gangs' appeared in *This Vision Thing*, Melbourne Poets Union, 2004.

Joan Kerr's 'All places are distant from Heaven alike' appeared in *This Vision Thing*, Melbourne Poets Union, 2004.

Andy Kissane's 'Loaves and Days' appeared in *Five Bells*, Vol. 10 (1), Summer 2003.

Peter Kocan's 'Name' appeared in *The Yellow Star of Life*, 2003.

Michael Ladd's 'A Vegetative Life' appeared in *Rooms and Sequences*, Salt Publishing, 2004.

Andrew Lansdown's 'Distress' appeared in *Studio*, Autumn 2004.

Anthony Lawrence's 'The Deep Scattering Layer' appeared in *The Sleep of a Learning Man*, Giramondo, 2004.

Cath Lee's 'The Planets' appeared in *Quadrant*, July–August 2004.

Ray Liversidge's 'Baudelaire the Bricklayer' appeared in *Obeying the Call*, Ginninderra Press, 2003.

Kate Llewellyn's 'The Clairvoyant' appeared in *The Weekend Australian*, 10–11 April 2004.

Miriam Lo's 'Farmgirl Marries' appeared in *My Cat Cannot Have Friends in Australia*, Five Islands Press, 2004.

Kathryn Lomer's 'Potato Cutters' appeared in *Extraction of Arrows*, UQP, 2003.

Yve Louis's 'Oysters in Gravey' appeared in *Blue Dog*, Vol. 2 (3), June 2003.

Myron Lysenko's 'Sex at the Poetry Workshop' appeared in *Said the Rat!: Writers at the Water Rat*, Black Pepper, 2003.

Ian McBryde's 'Stalingrad Briefing, 1943' appeared in *Domain*, Five Islands Press, 2004.

Shane McCauley's 'The Dissolution of a Fox' appeared in *Quadrant*, October 2003.

Dennis McDermott's 'The Up Train' appeared in *Dorothy's Skin*, Five Islands Press, 2003.

Paul Mitchell's 'Get the Word' appeared in *Minorphysics*, Interactive Publications, 2003.

Rod Moran's 'My Daughter Reading' appeared in *Quadrant*, June 2003.

Kevin Murray's 'The Ravenna Job' appeared in *Jaywalking Blues*, Domain Press, 1999.

Les Murray's 'The Cool Green' appeared in *The Times Literary Supplement*.

Geoff Page's 'Algebra' appeared in *Quadrant*, November 2003.

Christine Paice's 'Drama' appeared in *Quadrant*, May 2004.

Sheryl Persson's 'En Espana' appeared in *Blue Dog*, Vol. 2 (3), June 2003.

Dorothy Porter's 'The Ninth Hour' was commissioned for the *Last Words* concert performed by the Australian Chamber Orchestra, March 2004.

David Rowbotham's 'The Day of Singing Bells' appeared in *The Weekend Australian*, 21–22 August 2004.

Philip Salom's 'The Family Fig Trees' appeared in *Said the Rat!: Writers at the Water Rat*, Black Pepper, 2003.

Andrew Sant's 'Saxophone in a Pawnbroker's Window' appeared in *Tremors: New and Selected Poems*, Black Pepper, 2004.

Shen's 'Belief in Ghosts' appeared in *Blue Dog*, Vol. 2 (3), June 2003.

Craig Sherborne's 'Suburban Confidential' appeared in *Antipodes*, 2003.

Alex Skovron's 'Dreams of Dead Poets' appeared in *Said the Rat!: Writers at the Water Rat*, Black Pepper, 2003.

Andrew Slattery's 'Decision' appeared in *Love & Other Ways to Pass the Time*, Arrangement Media, University of Newcastle, 2004.

Vivian Smith's 'Friends and Ancestors' appeared in *Antipodes*, June 2004.

Sue Stanford's 'Rosellas' appeared in *This Vision Thing*, Melbourne Poets Union, 2004.

Maurice Strandgard's 'The King of Prussia Reveals' appeared in *Loneliness*, Five Islands Press, 2003.

John Tranter's 'Journey' appeared in *Studio Moon*, Salt Publishing, 2003.

Walter Vivian's 'A Steam-driven Computer' appeared in *Quadrant*, September 2004.

Samuel Wagan Watson's 'king' appeared in *Smoke Encrypted Whispers*, UQP, 2004.

Chris Wallace-Crabbe's 'Boleyn, Tourist' appeared in *Space*.

Meredith Wattison's 'Mr Waterfeet' appeared in *The Nihilist Line*, Five Islands Press, 2003.

Jen Webb's 'What the Pumpkin Knows' appeared in *Proverbs for Sierra Leone*, Five Islands Press, 2004.

John West's 'Mrs Jackson' appeared in *Quadrant*, June 2004.

Ouyang Yu's 'Far and Near' appeared in *New and Selected Poems*, Salt Publishing, 2004.